"*The Teen Girl's Survival Guide* is packed with powerful skills to help you develop and grow healthy relationships and positive connections. It helps you to identify and build on the skills you already have, and to discover and try out new ones along your journey of self-discovery, as you figure out who you are and where you fit in. The best part of the book is the wisdom and experience of actual teens in their own words—teens who really 'get it,' and can help you navigate social landmines and take your connectedness to the 'next level!'"

—**Dzung Vo, MD**, author of *The Mindful Teen*

"In *The Teen Girl's Survival Guide*, Lucie Hemmen uses a down-to-earth and engaging format to help readers manage critical teen issues, from social media stress to friend communication to self-esteem and sound decision-making skills. Teens will enjoy the advice from older girls, quizzes, and self-awareness exercises on topics they grapple with in their everyday life, while supervising adults will take comfort in the wisdom and solid guidance provided for keeping girls on track for making safe social choices."

—**Lisa M. Schab, LCSW**, psychotherapist and author of
The Self-Esteem Workbook for Teens, *The Anxiety Workbook for Teens*, and *Beyond the Blues*

"Hemmen guides the readers through every important challenge that teen girls face. She provides excellent tips and tools that will help them successfully navigate these critical years. Readers will not only survive, but thrive!"

—**Michelle Skeen, PsyD**, psychologist, author of *Love Me, Don't Leave Me*, and radio host of *Relationships 2.0 with Dr. Michelle Skeen* on KCAA 1050-AM

"*The Teen Girl's Survival Guide* nails the challenging and emotional nuances of growing up girl. The tips and tools Hemmen suggests are refreshingly honest, wise, and heartfelt. I look forward to sharing this resource with teens, parents, and educators."

—**Julia V. Taylor, MA**, author of *The Body Image Workbook for Teens, Salvaging Sisterhood*, and *Perfectly You*; and coauthor of *G.I.R.L.S. (Girls in Real Life Situations)* and *The Bullying Workbook for Teens*

"Lucie Hemmen's book provides ten fantastic tips that will help any teen girl thrive more in her life. The quizzes in each chapter are fun to take, and help to focus both on strengths and areas to work on. This book gives invaluable guidance on how to navigate the exciting and challenging world of social media."

—**Jennifer Shannon, MFT**, clinical director at the Santa Rosa Center for Cognitive-Behavioral Therapy, and author of *The Shyness and Social Anxiety Workbook for Teens*

"Hemmen provides girls with an invaluable resource, a guide for helping them handle tough interpersonal situations while helping them improve their self-esteem. Hemmen positions herself as a mentor and therapist by talking to readers on their level, which is so important. Readers will connect to the real girls' stories, and learn from the advice and tools Hemmen seamlessly weaves in through the chapters. I recommend this book for anyone working with teen girls, adolescents, and their parents. A must-have on bookshelves."

> —**Emily Roberts, MA, LPC**, psychotherapist and author of *Express Yourself*

"Finally, the guidebook to adolescence so many women I know wish they'd had, but can now offer their daughters, patients, students, and friends."

> —**Christopher Willard, PsyD**, author of *Child's Mind* and *Mindfulness for Teen Anxiety*, Cambridge Health Alliance/ Harvard Medical School

the *i*nstant help solutions series

Young people today need mental health resources more than ever. That's why New Harbinger created the **Instant Help Solutions Series** especially for teens. Written by leading psychologists, physicians, and professionals, these evidence-based self-help books offer practical tips and strategies for dealing with a variety of mental health issues and life challenges teens face, such as depression, anxiety, bullying, eating disorders, trauma, and self-esteem problems.

Studies have shown that young people who learn healthy coping skills early on are better able to navigate problems later in life. Engaging and easy-to-use, these books provide teens with the tools they need to thrive—at home, at school, and on into adulthood.

This series is part of the **New Harbinger Instant Help Books** imprint, founded by renowned child psychologist Lawrence Shapiro. For a complete list of books in this series, visit newharbinger.com.

the
teen g*irl's
survival guide

10 tips for **making friends, avoiding drama & coping** with **social stress**

LUCIE HEMMEN, PнD

Instant Help Books
An Imprint of New Harbinger Publications, Inc.

Publisher's Note

This publication is designed to provide accurate and authoritative information in regard to the subject matter covered. It is sold with the understanding that the publisher is not engaged in rendering psychological, financial, legal, or other professional services. If expert assistance or counseling is needed, the services of a competent professional should be sought.

Distributed in Canada by Raincoast Books

Copyright © 2015 by Lucie Hemmen
Instant Help Books
An Imprint of New Harbinger Publications, Inc.
5674 Shattuck Avenue
Oakland, CA 94609
www.newharbinger.com

INSTANT HELP, the Clock Logo, and NEW HARBINGER are trademarks of New Harbinger Publications, Inc.

Cover design by Amy Shoup
Acquired by Jess O'Brien
Edited by Jean Blomquist

Library of Congress Cataloging-in-Publication Data

Hemmen, Lucie.
  The teen girl's survival guide : ten tips for making friends, avoiding drama, and coping with social stress / Lucie Hemmen, PhD.
      pages cm. -- (The instant help solutions series)
   ISBN 978-1-62625-306-3 (paperback) -- ISBN 978-1-62625-307-0 (pdf e-book) -- ISBN 978-1-62625-308-7 (epub) 1. Teenage girls--Psychology--Juvenile literature. 2. Social skills in adolescence--Juvenile literature. 3. Interpersonal relations in adolescence--Juvenile literature. I. Title.
   HQ798.H447 2015
   305.235'2--dc23
                                2015026339

Printed in the United States of America

21   20   19

15   14   13   12   11   10

Mom and Dad, this book is dedicated to you.

Thank you for supporting everything I do, everything I've ever done. And for giving me the confidence and love to explore adventures like this one.

Contents

Acknowledgments

I am so lucky to be permitted into the lives of my teen girl clients—to bear witness to their experiences and to reflect what I observe. Sometimes venting occurs, sometimes raking through the leaves of their overstimulating lives, sometimes collaborating on ideas, possibilities, and solutions. I acknowledge teen girls and young women for providing the inspiration and the expertise that created this book.

With deep appreciation, I acknowledge my friends and family for supporting me in all the ways that sustain me. Beloved Beth, Andrea, Carrie, Jesse, Patrick, Tom, Heidi, Line—thank you for your support. I thank my endlessly enthusiastic sister, Cara, and nieces, Cali and Emme; my wonderful mom and dad; my treasured girls, Marley Rose and Daisy Rain. If I met you in any other format, I would choose you to be exactly who you are in my life.

Also, a big thank you to Jean Blomquist for her diligent editing and Jess O'Brien for stimulating momentum for this book. Thank you Manasa Grossman and Tyler Walicek for contributing to quiz creation. Your youthful perspectives were a big help. Joanna Doubleday, bless you for your enduring commitment to my online existence.

introduction

Welcome to The Teen Girl's Survival Guide!

This is a book about making your social life a success because having friends and feeling connected is important to you. While that seems like it should be easy, in the teen years, life is complicated. With a little support from *The Teen Girl's Survival Guide*, you'll be able to create more of the social life you want, with fewer complications.

While guys tend to think of high school as a requirement they have to fulfill, girls think of each day as a series of social interactions that either go well and feel good—or don't! "My whole mood seems to depend on what's going on socially" is a common teen girl complaint.

The good news is that social preoccupation, and the turmoil that goes with it, is completely normal. Whether you know it or not, most girls want the same thing: to feel liked and accepted within a secure group of friends they can feel comfortable with. This book will help you with that in two major ways:

1. It will help you increase the *quantity* of your social connections.

2. It will help you improve the *quality* of your social connections.

The best part about this book is that the tips come from the real experts: teen girls! Older teens who have learned a lot—often the hard way—and college girls outside the bubble of high school give their best advice to create this survival guide for you.

By the time you've read each chapter, you will have skills, strategies, and a solid understanding of how to make your social life come alive. To help you through the process, this book invites you to make personal lists, answer questions that help you self-reflect, and even take fun quizzes that help you get to know yourself better. While this can be done on a piece of paper, many girls have found that writing in a separate "tips notebook" works really well. Girls who use a journal or note-book for their "tips" work say it allows them to stay organized and go back to things they've written as a reminder of what they've worked on and how they've grown.

Notice that this survival guide is not a book on how to be "popular," and there's a reason for that. The reality is that many of the so-called "popular" girls aren't actually socially success-ful. Social success isn't about being well-known. It isn't about having as many people as possible following you on social media or talking about what they like or hate about you behind your back.

Social success is about *more* than being well-known. When you're socially successful, you feel good about yourself and your relationships. You feel confident in your ability to extend yourself, make connections, nurture relationships, and resolve conflicts.

If you want to feel good, authentic, and connected to plenty of people—*and* you want at least a handful of those relationships to feel mutually trusting and fun and rich—this book is for you!

tip 1

Know What You Bring to the Party

The first tip for social success comes from Carrie, who cringes when she looks back at her freshman year in high school. Carrie feels strongly that wanting a great social life requires knowing what you "bring to the party." When you recognize and feel good about the qualities that make you a special person and a good friend, you have a strong start toward social success.

According to Carrie:

Not knowing who you are and what you have to offer either makes you insecure, so you hold yourself back socially, or it makes you way too open to going along with the crowd because you want to fit in. When you know what you really have to offer people—what you "bring to the party"—you have the confidence you need to make good friends and mainly good decisions.

It's true that as you develop a sense of yourself and what you offer, you feel more confident in social situations. With more confidence, you can move *toward* social opportunities instead of away from them.

To illustrate this point, imagine you have this dream:

You are walking toward a giant door of a mansion. You hear noises from a party going on inside. You open the door, but you feel kind of strange, like you're not sure you're at the right place. You're not sure you're invited, or what exactly is going on inside. As the big door swings open, you stop, frozen in your footsteps. You are speechless and motionless as you behold the most amazing costume party you've ever seen. There are awesome costumes everywhere, and people interacting.

You wake up—in a sweat—mostly incoherent and pointlessly wondering, *Wait, what happened next? Did I join in? Did I even have a costume on? Who was I?*

Sound like one of your super-weird dreams? The party in the dream symbolizes your social life. It's a social situation that you're entering into. While your actual social life is probably not as amazing as your dream costume party, it will involve bringing yourself to situations where people interact. Key words: Bringing *yourself.*

Being unaware of your costume symbolizes being unaware of your qualities and what makes you special.

Now let's modify the dream:

Imagine you walk into that amazing party with full knowledge of your rocking costume. You chose it carefully and wear it with pride. You like your costume because it is a reflection of you. You are proud of it, and you want to share it with others—you expect they'll like it, too.

Suddenly, silence…as everyone turns to acknowledge your entrance. You gasp but then steady yourself, reminding yourself that you feel good about your costume, even proud of it. You move forward with optimistic expectation that meeting new people will be mutually interesting.

Tip 1 gets you started on social success by helping you create the experience above. You absolutely can be the girl who moves toward social opportunities with a blend of self-confidence and optimistic expectation. You can be the girl who knows what she brings to the party—and feel good about it!

You met Carrie earlier in this chapter and you'll get to know her better in the "Meet Carrie" section later. Her freshman year was like the first dream you read about. As Carrie herself notes, it wasn't an easy time, but it taught her a lot about the importance of knowing herself. By the time you complete this chapter, you will become more connected with yourself and what you have to offer—a connection that Carrie wishes she'd had when she was in high school.

As you work with this tip, keep in mind that as a teen girl, having a good sense of who you are doesn't come naturally. You are a developing human, which means you are a work in progress. Having a strong sense of self is rare at your age. That's because your teen years are a time when you figure out who you are and how you feel about people, academic subjects, music, activities, world issues, and life! You're not supposed to have clarity because you are learning and exploring and forming ideas about what you like, what suits you, and what choices and behaviors feel right for you.

"What you bring to the party" refers to qualities you have that are a deep part of who you are. Some of these qualities are still developing and some have been with you since you were little. When you have a sense of your qualities, you have important information about what makes you *you* and what makes you likeable to yourself and other people.

In this chapter, you will reflect, get to know yourself better, and establish a clear connection to your qualities. Carrie feels that if she had done that, she would have had the strength she needed to stay on course and make better decisions. Here is Carrie's story of getting through a tough time and what she learned from it.

✳ *Meet Carrie, Age 19*

The quote that inspires her:

> *For a moment, I felt like myself again. Not the new me,*
> *not the old me, just the real me.* —Leslea Tash

Back when I was in middle school, I had very little confidence and felt socially awkward. The transition from being a kid to being a preteen was just not a good time for me. Even though I wanted friends, I shied away from making them because I didn't have a sense that there was anything special about me—you know, that other kids would like. I had a friend Hailey who I'd had since kindergarten and we hung out, but I didn't really expand my social life very much.

The summer before freshman year, I decided things would be different in high school. I decided I'd make sure to come out of my shell and get a social life. I still didn't have a sense of anything good or unique about myself, but I vowed I would push myself to make new friends and have fun in high school.

Early in my freshman year, I made my first new friend in one of my classes. I acted friendlier than I really felt and she made it easy to talk to her, so we started hanging out. She had a big friend group that seemed really fun and social, and I liked being around everybody, especially at school.

Outside school didn't work out great because, as I learned, these kids were partyers who stole alcohol from their parents, sneaked out at night, and were just doing things that were a stretch for me. I was really scared and uncomfortable with all that at first, but I ignored it because I wanted to be accepted by them.

I did things I regretted that year. I regularly blew off my curfew and created a lot conflict with my parents. I had some problems with a couple of girls in the group because of stuff that happened when everyone was partying and—to give you the short version—there was a lot of unnecessary drama that went on. Again, I was more concerned about wanting friends than I was about losing myself, which I definitely was doing.

When my first progress report came, I realized how lost I was. I had always been a good student who cared about doing well, but I'd lost that—and my grades were terrible.

I hung out with Hailey less and she made other friends who seemed nice but, honestly, I didn't put much effort into getting to know her new friends. I felt too cool for them. One weekend, though, I had an overnight with Hailey and we did all the things we'd always done. We went thrifting and found cool stuff. We stayed up late and talked. We woke up in the morning and made banana–chocolate chip pancakes and watched a movie.

It was great, but it wasn't just about what we were doing. I felt like I was being myself. Hailey and I had always had long, deep talks about everything under the sun. We were always creative thinkers and great listeners for each other, and I'd forgotten how much that meant to me. She reminded me how excited we were for high school, wanting to do well in classes and make friends. I realized that she was still herself with her friend group. More importantly, I realized that even though I thought I was just changing in a normal way with my new friends, I was really forgetting who I was and what was important to me.

I went home and made a list of everything I could think of about the old me: that I care about school, and I like simple pleasures like going to the movies with friends and going thrift shopping and riding bikes and going out for food and reading and baking. I also wrote about all the qualities I have and can offer others. I wrote that I'm a good friend, and I'm supportive and patient with people. I wrote it all down, and writing it out made me feel better and more solid in a comforting way.

My tip for teen girls, especially those entering high school, is to get a sense of who you are and stay true to that. Or, if you lose yourself for any reason, because of a relationship or any kind of bad phase, to go back and find yourself.

If there's something you don't like about yourself, you can work on it, and if you want to grow and change yourself, that's cool, too—but never abandon or forget who you are. Don't absorb other people without hanging on to the qualities that make you special—that make you you.

Figuring It Out

On the road to learning who you are, lots of people go through hard, awkward, or just plain *bad* social phases. Even so, as with Carrie, both ups and downs can help you grow and refine your sense of self. This is especially true if you learn from challenging times and have a positive attitude about moving forward.

Many girls, however, get stuck in negative feelings about themselves and other people. If social success starts with understanding who you are and what you have to offer, you will need to let go of negative feelings before you move forward.

Letting Go

To make sure negativity is not weighing you down, take a moment to reflect on difficult phases you've been through socially. Do you remember times when you felt particularly uncomfortable, left out, or unhappy? Maybe negative feelings are focused on other people who didn't treat you well or with whom things went poorly. Notice the thoughts and feelings you have about yourself and other people.

Note: *Thoughts* happen in your head, from the neck *up*. *Feelings* happen in your body, from the neck *down*. Feelings are literally energy in your body. When feelings are painful or keep you from moving forward in your life, it's helpful to work with them so that you can release that negative energy.

These were Carrie's negative *thoughts* about herself in middle school:

* I wasn't cool enough.

* I didn't look "right," I didn't act "right."

* I wasn't as good as other kids.

* I was invisible to other people.

* I felt so awkward!

These were Carrie's negative *feelings* in middle school:

* I felt insecure.

* I felt anxious.

* I felt dread when I had to interact with other people.

* I felt awkward and uncomfortable.

This is Carrie's perspective now:

* I feel tenderness for the person I was in middle school.

* I now believe that I'm neither above nor below anyone.

* I don't worry about comparing myself to other people.

* I don't worry about being cool.

* I make sure to stay on track with liking myself and acknowledging myself so that I stay confident and enjoy getting to know other people.

When she reflected back on her negative thoughts and feelings, Carrie was able to open her heart to herself and get perspective.

Your Turn: Thoughts and Feelings About Yourself

Following Carrie's example, write down thoughts and feelings you have about yourself. You can write your responses on a piece of paper or in your tips notebook.

Take a look at what you wrote. Now it's time to let negative thoughts and feelings go so that you can move forward and create the positive experiences you want.

Clear Negativity

Letting go of negative thoughts and feelings is like cleansing your mind, body, and soul in preparation for goodness and positive experiences. While it's important to honor all your feelings and experiences, you don't need to carry them around forever. If you do, they will negatively affect your confidence in yourself and other people. This exercise will help you clear negative energy.

Try This: Replacing Negative Energy with Positive Energy

Teen girls who have tried this exercise say it helps replace negative energy with positive energy and optimism.

- Find a place where you have privacy and feel comfortable.

- Sit, close your eyes, and take three long, slow breaths.

- As you inhale, take in loving, healing energy toward yourself.

- As you exhale, let go of any negative energy, pain, or sadness.

- Continue to breathe in (take in love and healing energy) and breathe out (release negative energy, pain, or sadness) for as long as you want. Even one minute will prepare you for the next part of this exercise.

Now imagine some version of yourself sitting in front of you and follow the instructions below. Choose the you that you were during a difficult social phase. Carrie chose her middle school self. (She also did this exercise a second time picturing her high school freshman self.)

- Picture what you looked like, maybe what you were wearing and the way you styled your hair. As you hold this image of yourself, generate feelings of love for the girl you were—the girl who wanted to be liked and accepted.

- Holding the image of yourself before you, take five long, slow breaths. Each time you inhale, imagine breathing love and kindness into your heart. Each time you exhale, imagine your heart beaming that love toward the girl you were—the image of yourself sitting in front of you.

- As you inhale, feel the air come into your nose. Imagine you are heating the air with the warmth in your heart. As you exhale, imagine directing a magical beam of sparkling light toward the girl who sits before you.

- Imagine the energy healing her and restoring her to a state of peace and well-being.

- Tell the girl that you love her and that you plan on moving forward to create a solid, satisfying social life for both of you.

- Wrap your arms around her and hug her until she melts into your heart, where you will hold her safely and with great love.

Feel free to do this exercise any time you need to clear away negative feelings about yourself. Also, feel free to modify it in any creative way that you choose. No matter what you feel bad about, remember that beaming love to yourself will help things get better.

You can also use this exercise to clear away negative feelings you have toward a person, people, or even situations that have negative energy for you. Just picture that person, those people, or that situation, then beam love and kindness toward the one(s) with whom you want to clear negative energy.

It is never helpful to hold negative thoughts and feelings toward yourself. If you've made mistakes, figure out what went wrong, be kind and understanding toward yourself, and decide how you will handle things differently in the future. Forgive yourself, and move forward.

No good comes from punishing yourself with negativity. It hurts you *and* your ability to create the social success that you deserve.

Create Positivity

Now that you've cleared some negative thoughts and feelings, why not create some positive momentum? Learn to think gently about yourself and other people. This is crucial to social success.

For example, instead of:

Seventh grade was horrible. I was an awkward dork and had no friends.

Change to:

Seventh grade wasn't my best year, but I'm older now, I've learned a lot, and I have more power to make my social life better.

Here are more positive thoughts to try:

* Life gets better and better for me because I'm a good person and I'm always growing, changing, and improving.

* I have a lot of wonderful qualities that I can share with other people.

* There's a lot to like about me. I will remember that as I move through my day. I like me and other people will, too.

* It's normal to have hard times, but I'm always learning and I'm excited about moving forward.

* I accept that other people also change and often move on from the hard stages they go through.

* I feel more confident all the time. I like practicing positive thinking.

Your Turn: Positivity Boost

Think of more positive thoughts and write them down on a piece of paper or in your tips notebook. You can even write them on colorful 3 by 5 index cards and place them throughout your room. Imagine grabbing your socks tomorrow morning and seeing a neon orange card that reminds you that life is getting better and better.

One teen girl practiced this thought: *My life is getting better and better. I am becoming more and more confident every day.* As she practiced this thought, she concentrated on really feeling it as true and letting that feeling register deeply in her mind as well as in her body. She was shocked by how much her life began to change, as if by magic, from this simple practice. It's true that the more you practice positive thoughts and feelings, the more it becomes your "new normal." Give it a try!

What You Bring

Now that you've cleared negativity and are creating a new habit of positive thinking, you are ready to work on identifying what you have to offer socially. Knowing what's special about you gives you an idea of what you have to offer friends—or, as the chapter title says, "what you bring to the party." Some girls find it difficult to acknowledge their good qualities. There are two common reasons girls may overlook or disregard their strengths and good qualities. Can you relate to either?

Reasons Girls Overlook Their Good Qualities:

1. Being hard on yourself—self-critical—is a habit for you. You focus on what you consider to be your flaws and weaknesses.

2. You are more focused on what *other* people think of you than on what you think about yourself.

If you can relate to either or both of these reasons, it's okay—it's good to know what you need to work on. It's easy to get into negative habits and patterns, and the first step to improving them is to be aware of them. Then you can replace them with practices that help you create better habits.

Connecting with What You Like About Yourself

Let's get you connected (or reconnected) to the qualities you like and appreciate about yourself. One way of doing this is to name the qualities you liked in yourself as a young girl.

When asked to remember what she was like as a young girl, Carrie answered this way:

When I was nine and ten, I remember climbing trees, loving nature, and making up games to play with the neighbor kids. I loved time with friends and family. I remember starting my own business as a dog walker, and I got paid for walking and washing the neighborhood dogs. (Laughs.) I guess I had a good business mind. I was a carefree kid—very loving and confident.

When asked to remember what she enjoyed as a young girl, Carrie added:

I also enjoyed art, making people laugh, singing, and making up songs.

Your Turn: Remembering Your Younger Self

What were you like around age nine, ten, or eleven? These are often years when girls feel very powerful, and that's why they are a good focus for this exercise. You can, however, use another age if you prefer. Choose an age when you felt "large and in charge," and on a piece of paper or in your tips notebook, write down as much as you can remember about yourself then.

When you are through writing about yourself as you were then, look at what you wrote and identify those positive qualities that are still true for you. Place a star by anything you want to reconnect with and think of ways you can reclaim these treasured aspects of yourself.

Pay particular attention to how you feel when you focus on the girl you were. She is still with you today, even though you may have forgotten about her. She is the person you were before you began to worry about changing yourself in order to "fit in" or "be liked" by others. Reconnecting with her good qualities will help you feel more fully your true self.

Try This: Collect Five Good Things

This is a favorite exercise among teen girls. In this exercise, you will get insight into yourself by interviewing people in your life that know you and love you. The exercise is very simple: Ask at least three people in your life to list five things they appreciate about you.

Make sure to only ask people who care about you and who you can trust to take this assignment seriously. Aunts, uncles, friends, parents, teachers, or coaches can be good choices.

One girl wanted to ask her cousins and a friend. She texted them the question because she felt more comfortable doing that than asking them face-to-face. She said she was working on an exercise and needed their help to complete it. The info they texted back was surprising and helpful. She would have never known some of the qualities they appreciated about her.

Your Turn: Reflections on Five Good Things

On a piece of paper or in your tips notebook, write the comments you received about what others appreciate about you. Take some time to reflect on those comments, and then write down what you learned from them.

You can go back and read them whenever you feel lost about who you are and what you have to offer. When she did this exercise, Carrie wrote:

People who know and love me appreciate that I am smart, kind, and funny. The word thoughtful *came up twice in the feedback I got. I didn't realize that thoughtfulness was one of my qualities, but now I will appreciate that and even build on it. One person said I was sincere, and I like that word and its meaning. I guess it's true that I'm sincere, and I like that about myself.*

Being in Good Company—with Yourself!

Great job finishing Tip 1: Know What You Bring to the Party! Hopefully you can walk through your life now with a greater sense of your special qualities so that whether you're alone or with other people, you feel in good company with yourself. You are officially ready to move on to Tip 2: Leave Your Comfort Zone, where Bella shares her story.

Just-For-Fun Quiz: Find Your Flower Power

What best describes you? Write your answers on a piece of paper or in your tips notebook.

1. You could be described as

   A. friendly, optimistic, and cheerful.

   B. calm, sweet, and very personable when people get to know you.

   C. energetic, creative, and a little wild from time to time.

2. You are happiest

   A. being creative and outrageous with lots of other creative and outrageous people.

   B. with warm, loving, caring people who can engage with you in a positive way.

   C. alone, in an absorbing activity, or with one or two other people who are on your level. Loud people make you uncomfortable.

3. You are

   A. good with yourself alone, in small groups, or in big groups.

   B. really happy in a group of lively, expressive, creative people, which is more comfortable to you than one-on-one interactions.

   C. happy with alone time, time with family, and time with friends with whom you feel a depth of connection.

4. You love

   A. art, baking, or any activity or project that allows you to focus on being precise and skillful.

   B. interacting with others, supporting good causes, spreading good vibes, and developing strong bonds.

C.   acting, performing, dancing, and expressing yourself in general.

5.   When it comes to communicating,

   A.   you've been known to talk loudly, and your interactions (such as greeting a friend) are often enthusiastic and passionate.

   B.   you seldom talk loudly, but you're a good, effective communicator when you want to be. Encouraging and supporting other people is your communication specialty.

   C.   you talk when you have something to say. Talking is much easier for you when you're in a comfortable environment. If you're not comfortable, you may choose to say nothing.

6.   When it's time to recharge your energy,

   A.   your first choice is to recharge with other people. You don't really feel like you need much alone time to recharge.

   B.   your first choice is alone time with a good book, a show under your coziest blanket, or a quiet activity.

   C.   you like a little nap or rest, but afterward, you're ready to reengage with people.

7.   When it comes to dealing with difficult people,

   A.   you shut down and withdraw. That person may or may not get another chance with you.

   B.   you will try to talk to the person and work it out. If the person can't meet you at your level, you will focus instead on people who are more like you.

   C.   you may make a joke to let them know they've crossed a line, or you may give them blunt feedback so that they get the point.

SCORING

Add up your points.

1. A = 3 B = 1 C = 5

2. A = 5 B = 3 C = 1

3. A = 3 B = 5 C = 1

4. A = 1 B = 3 C = 5

5. A = 5 B = 3 C = 1

6. A = 5 B = 1 C = 3

7. A = 1 B = 3 C = 5

21–35 points: You are a wildflower.

Wildflowers are big, colorful personalities that like to be active and creative with other people. While wildflowers often hang out with other wildflowers, they also appreciate all kinds of other people. Diversity is interesting for wildflowers, who are also quite expressive and sometimes "out there." Because of their love for self-expression, wildflowers are often performers. They may be involved in drama, dance, improv comedy, or some other performing art.

Wildflowers aren't good with boredom, and may get in trouble if not optimally engaged. They sometimes trample over boundaries with other people, which can cause a bit of social chaos. It's hard for wildflowers to disappoint or upset other people because they generally like to entertain and make others happy.

If you're a wildflower, don't forget to rest, get some alone time, and take care of your responsibilities in life. Don't neglect things like school, and be sure to nurture important family relationships. If you're alone with a parent or sibling, give your phone a break and work on being present for a deeper connection. Be a good listener and ask questions to balance the breadth in your life with depth.

15–20 points: You are a sunflower.

As a sunflower, you gravitate toward all things warm, loving, friendly, uplifting, meaningful, and positive. You are an extraordinarily warm person and are at your best when your face is pointed toward the warmth of the sun—the warmth of life.

Communication is a natural ability for sunflowers, and they love other people they can talk about life with. Although sunflowers don't love conflict, they tend to take a breath and move through it as thoughtfully and effectively as possible. Many of their relationships are long-term and very close due to their communication skills.

Sunflowers can be alone or with others. They tend to have close family relationships, and enjoy doing fun things with family and friends. Sunflowers need to make sure they balance social time with quiet. Journaling is a great activity and self-care practice for sunflowers because it helps them balance their focus on other people with focus on themselves. If you are a sunflower, consider creative journaling as a way to stay close to yourself and your feelings.

7–14 points: You are a rose.

Roses are beautiful souls, both alone and in bouquets—groups of other people. They are grounded, caring, careful, and deep. Some may assume they are serious, but that's only before you really get to know a rose.

If you are a rose, you don't open up unless you feel comfortable. To know you is definitely to love you, but you are careful about who gets to know you. You are very environment-sensitive, meaning that under the right conditions, you blossom and open up to your full, amazing potential. If things don't feel right or someone rubs you the wrong way, you shut down.

A strength of roses is that they are good with themselves and enjoy their alone time. As a rose, you like solo activities that challenge your patience and skill—both of which you have plenty of. You like your time with special people, but after socializing for a while, you crave alone time to regroup and relax.

A great skill for you to work on is to make sure you speak up when you need to. Roses may prefer to let a storm pass without communication, which is fine sometimes, but not always. Sometimes you need to speak up and let people know how you feel about something or tell people when they've upset you. Take baby steps toward this goal so you can help people know how to treat you!

tip 2

Leave Your Comfort Zone

You will notice in life that it's often the outgoing people who seem to make things happen. It's wonderful to be kind and smart and talented, but if you have those qualities without making efforts to share them, you and your qualities stay confined to a small zone of experience.

While small zones, such as your family and a few friends, are wonderful in many ways, it's human nature to want more—more people, more experiences, more adventures, more fun, and more connection in your life.

Tip 1: Know What You Bring to the Party helped you to clarify who you are and what you have to offer. Hang on to what you learned about yourself and add to the list as you grow and change as a person. Be clear and connected to the qualities that make you special. Your list of qualities will be home base for you and will help you expand toward more opportunities, social and otherwise.

Now it's time to take steps toward sharing your qualities. To do that, you'll need to leave your comfort zone a bit. If you don't consider yourself outgoing, that's okay. You can still be a person who makes things happen. Think of being *outgoing* as the willingness to *go out* of your comfort zone.

As you know, your comfort zone is any place you feel entirely comfortable, a place of security where you don't need to push yourself at all. It can involve people, places, or situations that make you feel at ease. In your comfort zone, you can relax, rejuvenate, and take a break from "trying" or making great effort—it's a stress-free zone.

For many teen girls, their bedrooms are their comfort zones. You may not care that your bed is unmade and you have clothes on the floor. It's your sanctuary—the place where you can lie down and let go of the pressure you absorb all day.

You might have a different comfort zone, or even multiple comfort zones. Some girls say it's a friend's home or being with a group of well-established friends. Some say it's time they spend with grandparents or other family members or even pets. Maybe you share a commitment or an activity with a group of friends and that represents your comfort zone. No matter who or what defines your comfort zone, everyone can agree that the feeling you get when you're in it is great.

In the last chapter you met Carrie, who bolted out of her comfort zone because she wanted to make friends and be accepted. In doing so, she strayed too far and got involved in situations she later regretted.

As Carrie shared, she was "scared and uncomfortable" with what her new friends were doing, but she wanted to be liked and accepted by them. For sure, Carrie's experience is an example of abandoning your comfort zone unwisely. Fortunately, her sleepover with Hailey offered Carrie a wake-up call that helped her realize how far she had gotten from her comfort zone. Carrie thought she was moving toward social acceptance, but as it turned out, she landed up to her eyeballs in chaos and drama.

Avoid giant leaps out of the comfort zone and go with a slow and steady approach; it'll feel better and get better results. For example, you might choose to try small steps, or "field trips," out of your comfort zone that are safe and lead to growth instead of fear and discomfort.

This tip will introduce many such small and safe field trips. These baby steps will give you practice in the social bravery you will need to leave your comfort zone. This tip will lead the way. And to get you started, Bella shares how she left her comfort zone to create the social life she really wanted.

✱ *Meet Bella, Age 19*

The quote that inspires her:

> *Bravery is being the only one who knows you're afraid.*
> —Franklin P. Jones

Bella is a college sophomore who learned how to leave her comfort zone in her junior year of high school. She's excited to share this tip with you because she hopes you will learn this social lesson earlier than she did.

My first two years of high school were not much fun for me. I came from a small private K–8 school where I never had to try to make friends. We all knew each other, and so my skills at friend-making were zero by the time I entered a big, public high school. I don't know what I was thinking would happen, but I guess I thought I would magically have people to hang out with—which definitely did not happen.

I stuck with the few friends I already knew because it was low stress, but I was frustrated because I actually wanted to make new friends, too, and get out of my rut. I think I've always been a play-it-safe kind of girl, which is good in some ways because I'm responsible and don't get into trouble. But playing it safe is also restrictive, because putting yourself out there is what it takes to have a social life—a life in general, I think.

Looking back, I had opportunities to get out and meet people during my first two years of high school, but I either didn't take them or I turned them down. I could have gone to football games or other school events, but I never made the effort. And the few times I got invited to things—not formally but just "Hey, you wanna go?"—I found reasons not to go. I think I wanted to avoid feeling uncomfortable.

A life-changing thing happened in my junior year—my mom took on a German exchange student. Her name was Nicola; she was one year younger than I was and went to high school with me. Nicola was great. She spoke really good English, was sweet and funny and fun, and taught me everything I needed to know about leaving my comfort zone.

Nicola was good at getting out of her comfort zone. She was just turning sixteen and was out of her own country, so that tells you a lot. She wanted to have a full experience being with us and saw opportunity everywhere. That was the first bizarre thing for me because I didn't see opportunity anywhere. I was stuck in my comfort zone.

She would look up fun stuff to do online or in the local newspaper. She had an appetite for really offbeat stuff that I would have judged and pulled back from before I met her. For example, she loved cultural festivals and going to see local artists and musicians. She just had a huge appetite for life and living it fully..

The more I hung out with Nicola, the more she rubbed off on me. She approached people who seemed nice and cool and would ask questions and start talking. She would go to new places and look comfortable. If we went to a local concert or something, I would feel unsure, but she would walk in, figure things out—like where she wanted to sit or stand—and just make things happen. That made me realize how hesitant I was about everything I did. I always felt uncertain of showing up someplace new.

Nicola mostly used good judgment, so if something didn't feel right, she'd figure that out, too, and we'd leave—like a bonfire we went to one time that was out of control. We could both tell there was going to be drama. So we left and did our own thing. I feel like she taught me how to get out of my shell, out of my comfort zone, and life is so much more interesting when you do that!

I thought I needed to develop confidence before I could get out of my comfort zone. But as it turned out, I got out of my comfort zone and then I built confidence. It makes sense to me now: how can you build confidence if you don't stretch yourself, check out opportunities to do new things and meet new people, and find out you're fine—even better—outside your comfort zone?

Now my comfort zone is less rigid. When I got to college, I was uncomfortable, but I knew I could get comfortable if I put myself out there and met new people, checked out all the cool opportunities, and made efforts to get involved. That's how you make more of your life your comfort zone.

My tip for girls is that you have to leave your comfort zone to expand your social life. You need to be brave sometimes. Not dumb—don't do anything that doesn't feel right—but brave. Say yes to opportunities and make things happen for yourself.

Figuring It Out

In Bella's first two years of high school, she stayed in her comfort zone because even the thought of taking a social risk felt scary. Having Nicola come was like a fairy godmother blessing her with the perfect social coach! It's very helpful to hang out with someone who has mastered something you would like to learn.

In Bella's case, she learned that living life more fully required leaving her comfort zone and being more adventurous. What Bella did not expect is that her acts of bravery would bring her the confidence she always wanted.

Face the Fear

The first thing girls often feel when they think of pushing themselves to do new things is a spike of fear, nervousness, vulnerability, and self-doubt. Doing new things, meeting new people, and starting new activities often involves initial fears like these:

* What if I don't know what to do?

* What if people don't like me?

* What if I don't like them?

* What if I embarrass myself?

* What if I don't have anything to say?

* What if I'm uncomfortable?

All of those fear-based thoughts are completely normal. Almost everyone has them when they're trying something new, which is why it feels "risky."

There are times when fear gives you important information about being at risk in some way, in which case it's helpful. Remember Carrie sharing that she was "scared and uncomfortable" with the activities of her new friends? In Carrie's case, listening to her fear could have saved her from a lot of stress and chaos.

Other times, however, fear is a signal that you *feel* in danger, but the actual potential for danger is exaggerated by your mind. You may feel fear before joining a new activity or going to a school dance or hanging out with new people or trying to get to know someone better. In all of these cases, the actual potential for danger is low. The root of your fear is that you'll be uncomfortable. Feeling uncomfortable may not be fun, but it's not dangerous.

Make Friends with Discomfort

When you know that your fear is about discomfort and not actual danger, you have a choice: you can move out of your comfort zone toward a social opportunity, or you can stay in it and let the opportunity pass you by.

Learning to feel discomfort and yet pursue things that are good for you *in spite of your discomfort* is the heart of Tip 2: Leave Your Comfort Zone. Over time, you'll notice that you have a greater ability to handle discomfort and that your increased social bravery melts it away more quickly.

When you are ready to take those brave steps, instead of thinking, *No way. I can't do that—I'll be too uncomfortable*, think,

This could be a great experience. I'm nervous, but oh well—I'll get through it, and there's a good chance it will be worth the risk!

Here are some tips from teens on how they've made friends with discomfort:

Beth: I remind myself that other people can't read my mind and that my discomfort doesn't show.

Mara: I try to take deep breaths and relax, especially my shoulders. When my body relaxes, my mind tends to follow—it relaxes, too.

Talley: What I do is I pay attention to everything outside of myself. It makes me more present in the moment, and it distracts me from focusing on how uncomfortable I feel.

All of these teens agree that when they use their strategies, their discomfort fades after a short period of time.

Bottom line: When fear keeps you from taking risks that are safe and promote your personal and social growth, you are getting trapped in your comfort zone. Instead of staying safe by avoiding danger, you are staying comfortable by avoiding growth. Ultimately, that won't be very comfortable.

Field Trips

How often do you face the fear and take advantage of opportunities? If there's room for improvement, consider increasing your social bravery and planning more field trips that take you out of your comfort zone.

Some girls keep a log of their efforts. Here is an example from sixteen-year-old Maddie:

My Field Trips This Week

* Talked to the girl who sits next to me in bio.

* Said yes instead of no when Jules asked me to hang out with her volleyball friends.

* Plan on going to the game this Friday night.

* Plan to make an effort to talk to people at the game on Friday.

* Told my mom that I'll go to my dentist appointment on my own.

* Went to get gas with Dad and dealt with the whole process of pumping and paying.

Notice that Maddie's last two field trips had nothing to do with her social life. Even so, Maddie found that *all* of her field trips helped her build social bravery and confidence. So try some of your own.

Your Turn: Planning Your Field Trips

What field trips can you plan for yourself? Using Maddie for inspiration, come up with field trips that will help you expand your comfort zone. Write them down on a piece of paper and put the list somewhere where you'll see it, as a friendly reminder—or write them in your tips notebook and refer to your list often.

Fear and Your Brain

All of your feelings are important, and learning to work with them, instead of being controlled by them, gives you more personal power in your life. Fear is an especially important feeling that has allowed us to evolve as a species and survive on the planet.

As we evolved, our fear alarm signaled us to recognize danger in order to keep ourselves safe. However, the function of fear is not to keep us trapped. And even though the alarm came in very handy for our survival, in some situations we don't need to *obey* the fear response without some consideration. That's because sometimes the fear alarm goes off when there is the "danger" of discomfort, not actual danger. For example, feeling the fear that you will be awkward and uncomfortable if you go to a school dance is different than feeling the fear that you will die if you get into a car with someone who has been drinking alcohol.

You can give yourself credit for knowing what is actually danger or has strong potential for danger, and what is actually the fear of being uncomfortable. Most of the time, you will be able to tell the difference.

If you find yourself in a situation that doesn't seem dangerous at first but then becomes dangerous, take immediate steps to create safety for yourself. Some self-protection experts say the best thing to do when you sense any kind of trouble is "don't be *there*." In other words, get out now!

In Carrie's case, when she found herself in situations where she was "scared," she did have choices. Instead of staying in the situation, she could have told her friends that she was going home. She could have shared that she was uncomfortable with what was going on, *or* she could have kept that to herself. Either way, leaving the dangerous or potentially dangerous situation would have been a better choice for her.

Danger Zone

A lot of the harm, chaos, and drama that teenagers go through occurs when teens party with drugs and alcohol, sneak out at night, and put themselves in positions that have a high potential for danger. Leaving your comfort zone for those kinds of opportunities can hurt you and the trust you've built with the adults who care for you. In the bigger picture, teens often find that the fun they think they're going to have comes with too high a price.

But what about when your fear alarm goes off and there's no actual danger? What do you do when unreasonable fear pushes you back and traps you in your comfort zone?

How to Turn Off the Fear Alarm

Here are tips from three college girls who have experienced turning off the fear alarm so they can explore life beyond the comfort zone:

Marley: Honestly, I learned to "fake it 'til I make it." I am very social when I feel comfortable, but I am not one of those people who feels comfortable right away. What I figured out is that other people cannot see through me. I'm not that transparent and, even more importantly, other people are not as focused on me as I'm afraid they will be. They are thinking about other things.

Now I will walk into a room with people I don't know and act like I'm completely comfortable. I focus on relaxing my body and faking confidence. I try to engage in what's going on right away because otherwise I can stay too much to myself. People believe what they see. They're not psychic! Fake it 'til you make it and you won't be faking for very long. You will feel comfortable.

Georgie: I totally agree! That's what I've done, but also I've learned to say yes to new things, even when I want to stay at home and watch shows on my bed. My first reaction when I hear about some social thing happening is to think, *No—I don't want to go.* I hate feeling uncomfortable. I want to be cozy in my room, on my bed, chillin'. But I don't give in to that, unless I really need rest or I really know I won't like the activity. I stretch myself a lot, and I've been really happy with the results. I'm involved in a lot of college clubs and organizations and I've met so many cool people that I love. My tip is to say yes more often.

Natalia: Yes to both Marley and Georgie. My tip is to take little risks everywhere you can—risks that are safe, of course, and build your bravery. Before I left for college, my mom just had me take on more responsibilities to build my bravery. She had me make my own appointments, take my car in for service by myself, plan getting my wisdom teeth out, stuff like that. All of that was uncomfortable for me. I'd never even bought my own tampons before. Anyway, even though that stuff wasn't necessarily socially oriented, being brave anywhere transfers to being brave socially. I got two jobs over the summer and that helped me be brave because I had to sell myself. I also did some traveling and figured out all the details and stuff by myself. My tip is to practice acts of bravery anywhere you can.

Learn to Be Intrepid

The teen girls who have shared their stories and experiences encourage you to become more *intrepid* in your social life. (If you don't know what that word means, look it up. More and more it is describing *you*.) Now that all these new social skills have enabled you to safely leave your comfort zone, you might wonder, *What's next?* No worries. The next chapter, Tip 3: Increase Contact, has all the answers. Read on.

Just-For-Fun Quiz: Are You an Expander, a Maintainer, or a Retreater?

Write your answers on a piece of paper or in your tips notebook.

Let's say you find out that a friend has been saying bad things about you behind your back. How do you react?

A. Contact the friend in hopes of having a helpful conversation about what might be going on.

B. Think about it as best you can, maybe write about it in your journal, and let it go.

C. Stay at home, watch a movie, and try to forget what happened.

You're at a loud party with lots of people. What do you do?

A. Introduce yourself to a stranger, feeling intrigued by the opportunity to meet someone new.

B. Hang around the people that you already know, making conversation, but feeling a little awkward about the strangers around you.

C. Sit on the couch and play on your phone, thinking about leaving early.

Do you feel like there's a limit to how much you can socialize? How soon, if ever, do you get "burned out" on hanging out with people?

A. I *need* to be around people, or I start to feel restless.

B. I love seeing my friends, but after a couple hours, I need to recharge.

C. I'd rather not socialize at all. I'd prefer a Netflix binge.

When you think about the future, how do you feel?

A. Excited! Yes, the future is scary, but I see life as an adventure, and there are many experiences and adventures I have to look forward to.

B. A little freaked out, but I know that I can make things happen, one step at a time.

C. Terrified. I often feel overwhelmed with life already, and the future seems really intimidating.

SCORING

Add up your points.

A   = 1 point

B   = 2 points

C   = 3 points

4–6 points: You are an expander.

Expanders feel fear but respond to it by moving forward, toward what they want. Some expanders move forward without much thought, while others consider a strategy and move forward with care and consideration. If you are an expander, you may be the leader in your friend group because you're fun and you make things happen.

7–9 points: You are a maintainer.

The status quo is where you feel comfortable—you're good at keeping up existing relationships and remaining stable in your life. You're generally reliable, and can be counted on to be there for your friends. You greatly value the relationships you have.

10–12 points: You're a retreater.

Expanding yourself into social situations is stressful for you. You respond to stress by comforting yourself with distractions, such as spending time on your phone or other comforting habits. The idea of being more connected socially intrigues you, but you struggle to come up with the motivation and confidence to push through your fears. Working on leaving your comfort zone in order to build social experience will help you develop confidence. Retreaters become socially expansive as they move beyond their fears.

tip 3

Increase Contact

If you play soccer or another ball sport, you may have heard your coach encourage you to increase contact with the ball. If you hear "get to the ball, get to the ball, get to the ball" or "touch the ball," it's because your coach knows that the more you push yourself toward that darn ball, the more comfortable and confident and skillful you will become.

Some girls embrace the principle of getting to the ball, while others are more intrigued by the tiny, daisy-like weeds growing in the field. Either works fine when you're a little girl learning soccer, but it's time now to cultivate your inner "go getter," which means you go get the social contact you left your comfort zone for.

Whether you're developing athletic skills or reaching out to make new friends, it's normal to experience a feeling of awkwardness when you practice something new. As you learned from Tip 2: Leave Your Comfort Zone, your feelings don't have to hold you back. You can feel them and still move toward your goal.

Thankfully, awkward feelings disappear with steady practice, because the more you practice anything, the more comfortable you feel with it. And the more comfortable you feel, the more skillful you become at increasing contacts and friendships and widening your social comfort zone.

Learning the importance of leaving your comfort zone, and how to do it, was huge in Tip 2. In Tip 3, the new challenge is learning how to make contact with others once you've left it.

You will learn that as you push out the *boundaries* of your comfort zone, your comfort zone will keep expanding. And as you practice the strategies in this chapter, you will soon find that you're happier and better connected in all kinds of zones. Just as the "go getter" feels comfortable all over the field, like she belongs there, you will feel better in whatever environment you're in.

One girl learned to expand her social zone and make new contacts out of necessity when her family moved to a different state and she was faced with making friends in a new high school. Let's hear Lindsay's story.

✳ *Meet Lindsay, Age 18*

> *How wonderful it is that nobody need wait a single moment before starting to improve the world.* —Anne Frank

Lindsay is an eighteen-year-old high school senior. This tip comes from a lesson she learned when she was a sophomore.

> *When I was halfway into my sophomore year, my dad got a job in another state and I had to move. It was the worst possible thing at the time, but at this point in my life, I look back on it as a situation that forced me to grow.*

I've always moved a lot, more than other kids I know, but at sixteen it was so much harder because all I wanted was stability and a friend group that I could count on. It sucked for me because all of that got ripped away, and I found myself in a new school with tons of kids I didn't know.

I'm good at being outside my comfort zone because I've had experience moving and making peace with being an outsider until kids got used to me and I got used to them. But that was when I was younger, and as a teenager, I felt more intimidated and way more awkward.

The thing I know about awkwardness is that it feeds on itself, so every day at my new school I gave myself an assignment to reach out in some way. Every day I would literally force myself into making some kind of contact with other kids. For example, since I, for real, didn't know where I was going, it was a no-brainer to ask somebody who seemed approachable for directions to class. Then, when I was in class, it seemed obvious to ask the people sitting around me for information about the lessons, homework, teacher, and so on.

One thing I learned from changing schools so much is that if you give them a chance, lots of kids will give you help if you ask for it. And when you reach out for help, it gives them a chance to help you and meet you without feeling awkward themselves.

Another way I reached out was to see if anybody I met was interested in the same things I'm interested in—like clubs and after-school activities and stuff. I got all the information I wanted, plus I met some people who are also into music and art. One thing led to another, and I ended up with a nice little group of friends.

What I would want you—and all teen girls to know—is that unless you are eating your boogers in public, no one really knows how awkward anybody feels just by looking. You are not as exposed as you feel! I want younger teens to believe that because it's true. It took a while for me to realize that even though I felt like everyone could see how awkward I was, they really couldn't.

Anyway, I really recommend giving yourself assignments like the ones I tried because that worked for me. I made some new friends in the first week at my new school, and after the first month, I had plenty of girls to hang out with. Now as a senior, I have three best friends and a bigger group of guys and girls who are fun and definitely good, positive people to be around.

Figuring It Out

What about you? Do you make friendly contact with kids outside your comfort zone a lot? Or almost never?

Lindsay makes friendly contact *a lot!* For her, it means reaching out in small ways that show she is friendly. *Even when I don't think this person is going to end up being my best friend, I like to show that I'm a friendly person. I try to make eye contact and say, "Hi." I ask, "How's it going?" It sounds lame, but I smile at most people. It's just a habit with me and it makes me happy to be friendly and outgoing, not only with close friends but with just acquaintances.*

To get started with assignments, try to extend yourself to make connections five times a day.

Your Turn: Homework for Baby Steps

This assignment is not incredibly terrifying because you will start off by doing *little* things that help you extend yourself toward others—for example, smiling at someone in the hall or saying "Hi" to the person who sits next to you in class. Then, the next day, do five more things that extend you a bit more—maybe introduce yourself to someone you don't know or ask where to get info on a club or activity. Using Lindsay's experience as a guide, each day extend yourself five times by reaching out to others using small gestures to increase the number of people you feel comfortable with. List these gestures on a piece of paper or in your tips notebook.

- List the five things you'll do today.

- List five things that you do each day for the rest of the week.

- At the end of the week, reflect on what you've done and how you feel about it. Did you meet some new people or learn about new activities? Did it start to get easier to connect with people? What did you learn this week—about yourself and others?

Not all of these people will become your friends. You may not even want them to! What you do want is to have more people in your life that you feel familiar with and comfortable around. From there, friendships that you do want can evolve more easily and naturally.

Tips for Extending Yourself Socially

Making simple social extensions has worked well for many socially successful teens. Here is what some of them have to say about extending themselves:

Jadon: Be nice to everyone, but don't do it in a phony way. Make sure you feel real and then it will be more sincere. I think if people aren't real, other people can feel the fakeness, so I make sure to feel sincere before I try to connect with other people.

Caitlynn: I smile and say hi to people all day long, no matter where I am. I like to smile and pass on good vibes to people. School can be stressful and depressing, and being friendly to people, even if I don't know them, keeps my attitude positive.

Dani: I got really good at introducing myself to people. As a freshman in college, it saved me! I sat in my dorm room all alone and then decided to walk down the halls and say hey to all the people I passed with their doors open. It was hard at first, but then I realized kids wait around for other kids to take the initiative. Now, I barge in and just say, "Hey, I'm Dani" to get things going. Friendliness and warmth put other people at ease, and it puts me at ease too 'cuz when I'm pulled back, I feel worse, not better.

Mimi: There's this weird zone when you know someone through someone else or because you've seen each other around but you don't know them well enough to say "hi," or you don't think they will remember you. I used to be paralyzed with a lot of people because of that awkward zone. Then I learned to break through it by going up to people and saying, "Hi, I'm Mimi. I know who you are, but we've never officially met" or "Hi again. I've seen you (or met you)—I'm Mimi." Confronting the awkwardness and addressing it directly like that has worked great for me.

Kylie: My high school has an open campus, so asking people if they want to have lunch is a way to get to know someone better. It gives you a structure for hanging out so you feel more comfortable.

Avery: My best friends at my new school happened through connecting about schoolwork—and then expanding. Honestly, study groups or talking about schoolwork can be the first stepping stone to going off campus to get tea to hanging out on the weekends to really getting to know each other and becoming real friends.

Zaya: Complimenting opens doors, but I don't like to just compliment appearance or material things. I like to say things that are a little more meaningful, like complimenting someone on how positive they are or something.

Shannon: My thing is making study guides in class and posting them on social media for other kids in the class. People always appreciate it. Sometimes I get together with other kids and we make a study guide together. I made a good friend that way, actually.

Ruby: All the friends I have I pretty much made from class or from seeing them in activities. At my school, we are required to join a club or have an on-campus activity, and that ended up making me more comfortable with those kids, some of whom became my good friends. I would tell other girls to join activities and make social efforts in class, for sure.

Lily: I heard that kids hang out at this coffee shop near school, so I started going there and just saying hi and forcing myself to be friendly. Then I'd see some of those people in class or in the hallways, and I'd smile and say hi again until I built up a feeling like I actually knew some people.

Ava: My strategy is to throw myself into being friendly before I can think about it. If I think about what I want to say, I get self-conscious, so I just pretend I'm a Labrador and I go up to people in a friendly way. It's amazing how well this works. It's hard to resist a warm, friendly person.

Selena: I love hanging out with my friend Rachel because she's a total extrovert. I learn a lot from watching her. She just unselfconsciously walks up to people and starts talking to them. I've started to do the same thing with and without her. I've met way more people and life is just so much better when you feel you at least kinda know a lot of people.

Getting Started

The teens you heard from offer lots of ideas about simple social extensions that worked for them. However, most of the girls will admit that it took some time before they became comfortable reaching out—they had to be patient with themselves as they learned to do it. One tip that some of them offered as a way to get started was to notice what other people do to connect. Here are some examples of personal extensions you can try:

* Smile at someone.

* Say "How's it going?" or something similar.

* Say something school related: "Are you ready for this test?" "Do you understand this?"

* Issue a surface compliment: "I like your shoes." "That color looks so good on you." Surface-level compliments work great as icebreakers when you really don't know the person. (But don't give a compliment unless it's authentic.)

* Issue a more significant compliment: "You gave great feedback in class" or "You have a great attitude."

* Make a school-related inquiry: "You missed class last week. Are you okay?" or "Do you need to borrow my notes?"

* Make a non-school-related inquiry: "Did I see you at the mall over the weekend?" or "Aren't you on the volleyball team?" or "Are you friends with Wendy?" or "Did you used to take dance downtown?" or "Did you go to the game last night?"

* Issue a school-related invitation: "Do you want to study for the test together?" or "Should we get some people together and study for this test?" or "Want to work on this project together?"

✳ Issue a non-school-related invitation: "Do you want to hang out sometime?" or "Want to get some food after class?" or "I want to see a game. Can we meet before?"

Your Turn: Reflecting on Your Extensions

Now it's time to reflect on the extensions you've tried. Write your answers on a piece of paper or in your tips notebook.

• Make a list of extensions you have tried. What worked? What didn't?

• Make a list of extensions you are willing to try.

• Have you observed other people extending themselves? What seemed to work? What didn't?

• Have you observed extensions that you want to try?

There is no "one size fits all" approach to social success. You have to honor who you are and respect your personal timetable. Two teen girls, Juliana and Beth, tried personal approaches and each increased familiarity with a lot of new people. This is what they say about extending themselves:

Juliana: I am very shy, so I started with simple ways to connect with others. I worked on making eye contact, and smiling, and saying hi. I only did these three extensions, but I stuck with them and did them five times a day.

Beth: Friends who have known me for a long time would describe me as outgoing, but I have to really get to know people before I can be friendly. I chose a different extension every day and before long I was able to invite people to do stuff.

Humanity Extensions: Reaching Out to the World

Have you ever felt compelled to engage in a random act of friendliness? It could be as simple as giving a warm hello to the neighbor you pass, instead of pretending you don't see him or her. *Humanity extensions* are acts of friendliness and kindness that you take by extending to make contact with people outside the "bubble" of your everyday social habits. Humanity extensions can spontaneously erupt from the energetic feeling a great mood brings or from making a conscious effort, which then puts you in a good mood. Either way, humanity extensions are mood food for the "extender" as well as the receiver!

As you begin to feel comfortable reaching out at school, expand your zone in a bold way and think of the world around you as a great setting to practice social extensions. Making contact through extending yourself helps you feel confident and connected while making the world a kinder, gentler place for everyone.

Rewarding Contacts

Some of the teen girls who tried making contact through humanity extensions commented that their efforts not only made others happy, but made them feel uplifted as well. You might want to try some of the following humanity extensions to see the uplifting impact you can have on another person.

Try it when:

* You see an elderly woman at the grocery store, make some nice eye contact and smile.

* You pay for your muffin at the bakery, radiate a little extra kindness to the cashier.

* You hold the door open for the person entering a building behind you.

* You acknowledge a child for her red, sparkly shoes.

Goodness and positivity create more goodness and positivity. All your kind efforts, large and small, generate more goodness and connection for you.

One teen girl, Leah, has experienced many benefits from reaching out to others. This is what she has to say about utilizing positive extensions in her life:

Leah: I notice that when I'm moody or stressed, I live in my own bubble sealed off from other people. When I remember to do humanity extensions, I pop the bubble I'm in and get over myself. Small positive and random connections with other people make me feel better. You never know...the person you're nice to might be having the worst day of his or her life and maybe you just made it better.

My favorite humanity extension is to compliment people on their dogs, especially older people because their dogs mean so much to them. So when they walk their dogs, I say something nice about the dog or ask a question. Then they look so happy and tell me stuff about the breed or whatever. I learn something, but more than that, I can tell they are happy a teenager gave them the time of day and it makes me happy. I'm just getting in the habit of being friendly instead of in my own head.

Lots of teen girls say that humanity extensions have been a truly life-changing experience for them. They have noticed that when they act friendlier toward others, they feel better about themselves, other people, and life. One good thing just leads to another.

Your Turn: Humanity Extensions

Perhaps you are a person who already makes humanity extensions. Or maybe you've observed them made by others. Think about some of the humanity extensions you have made or have noticed, and make a list of them on a piece of paper or in your tips notebook.

Now make another list of humanity extensions you are willing to try.

As you repeat humanity extensions you've already made or try new ones, make a note of how your kind efforts make you feel and the reactions you notice from others.

Making Progress

As you work to increase contact with others, remember that life is a marathon and not a sprint. Be kind and patient with yourself as you make progress toward social success. Take your time. You will feel more comfortable making bigger extensions, such as issuing invitations, once you have more comfort and familiarity. That's why extensions such as setting up study groups or other school-related meetings often lead to making friends.

As you move forward in extending yourself toward others, notice your improvement and give yourself a pat on the back for your effort. After you have made the effort and increased the quantity of your connections, you will find it easier and more natural to take some of those connections to the next level: friendship.

To learn more about growing friendships, read on. In Tip 4: Nurture Connections, you'll see how one girl, Skye, helps grow the seeds of connection into a garden full of beautiful friendships.

Just-For-Fun Quiz: Which Household Pet Are You?

On a piece of paper or in your tips notebook, write yes or no for the following items to see which household pet you have more in common with. (Meow or woof?)

As a little girl (age eleven and younger), the following described me. I would rather…

- play on the computer than build a fort.

- go to someone's house for a play date than explore a new playground.

- move gracefully than move quickly.

- chill in my house than explore the neighborhood for fun and adventure.

- climb a tree than run or ride bikes.

- hang with one friend than hang with a group.

- be with quiet, calm people more than loud, big-personality types.

- find projects to do in the house than adventures outside of the house.

- color or play a game than perform a dance or song of any sort.

- play an instrument than be on a team of any sort.

- organize something than make a mess.

- observe an activity before jumping right in.

- miss out by taking too long to make a decision than make a quick decision and make a mistake.

- be polite and thoughtful than be the center of attention.

SCORING

Count up and total your yes and no answers.

If you answered mostly no, you're a dog—woof!

You enjoy your down time, but being out and about and seeing the world and other people really energizes you. You like doing things and being places. You tend to be affectionate and social. You have an easy time putting yourself out there, and often are a leader among your friends. Every now and then, you may get scolded for being thoughtless or reckless, which is hard for you because you prefer to make everyone happy.

Growth for you lies in becoming more thoughtful and conscious during your social interactions. You are already socially oriented. Now you can practice making social interactions more meaningful and purposeful. Pay attention to how you impact other people—an enthusiastic dog may jump on people to say "Hi" and fail to notice her muddy paw marks on their clothing. Bring a gentle awareness to other people's emotional experience and enjoy becoming more attuned to subtle nuances.

If you answered mostly yes, you're a cat—meow!

You love comforts like being home in a comfortable spot, reading, and engaging in chill activities. You are a great observer of people and notice things others may miss. When you're comfortable and in the mood, you like to interact with people, but you don't have an endless appetite for socializing. You are actually very happy in your own company or spending time with the people you're closest to. You don't tend to rub people the wrong way because you're a bit socially cautious and selective about letting people get to know you.

Growth for you will come from taking more risks. This doesn't mean acting crazy, but rather taking on new challenges that help you build life experience and confidence. What people, places, or activities can you add to your life? Also, if you enjoy solitary activities like art or writing, who might you share your work with? Sharing this part of you will help special people get to know you on a deeper level, and that will be a great feeling.

tip 4

Nurture Connections

As you continue to work on the tips you've learned so far, are you noticing anything new about yourself? Let's take a moment to appreciate your progress: you've gained a sense of who you are and what you have to offer other people, you are expanding your comfort zone, and you are increasing the number of people you make contact with daily.

It's time to take the next step, which is to deepen the *quality* of your connections by nurturing them. All of these efforts support you in getting yourself on the radar as a more social person.

The last chapter, Tip 3: Increase Contact, was very important in reaching this goal because increasing contacts is like planting seeds in your social garden. The more contacts you make, the more seeds you plant. If you want a garden full of beautiful flowers, you will need to plant many seeds. But to help those beautiful flowers grow, you can't just plant the seeds and forget about them. You must nurture them—water, weed, fertilize, and carefully tend them—so they grow healthy and strong. That's what happens when you nurture the contacts you've made—they can become healthy and strong relationships.

As you nurture connections with others, you will notice that positive things start happening: walls come down, fears melt away, confidence develops, and relationships bloom. Instead of walking around focused on yourself, you open up to the thoughts and ideas and company of other people. And life comes alive with new possibilities.

When you nurture the seeds you've planted—the contacts you've made—you give them the opportunity to grow into something more. In this chapter, older teens share how they've nurtured their connections to create deeper relationships. Skye is first to share her tip and the story of the ups and downs (and ups again) of her social life.

✱ *Meet Skye, Age 19*

I've learned that people will forget what you said, people will forget what you did, but people will never forget how you made them feel. —Maya Angelou

Skye is a sophomore in college who says her social success is largely due to the effort she puts into nurturing relationships. Just as a gardener puts love and care into growing flowers, Skye believes the love and care she puts into relationships creates friendships that are close and fulfilling. She is a big believer that *being* a good friend is the key to social success.

Even as a little girl, I always liked to be thoughtful with my friends. I was not one of those kids who was oblivious to others. I paid attention to people's feelings and I liked being able to make people feel happy and loved. I was like that with animals and old people, too. My mom says I'm generous with love.

When I turned fourteen, I went through a phase where I became insecure and stressed because my friends were changing a lot. Girls I'd known since kindergarten suddenly seemed really different and hard to relate to. I felt like everyone was boy crazy except me. It felt like all the ways we used to connect disappeared, and even though we knew each other, I stopped feeling comfortable.

It was a really hard time for me. It's weird feeling lonely when you're with people you know! For a while, I pulled away from social stuff. I spent more time with my family and my dog than with friends. It sounds depressing, but I needed that time away from how stressed out I felt socially.

After almost a year of that, I got sick of having no social life, so I gradually began to put more energy into building friendships. It felt harder than it did when I was younger, and I had huge flare-ups of self-doubt. Then I remembered that being a good friend was my secret to having good friends before, and the same thing was probably true now.

I started putting energy into the people around me. If there was someone in a class who seemed nice or interesting, I would put more energy into getting to know her. If there was a friend who I used to be close to that I missed, I would make efforts to try to reconnect. It took work because I was coming from about a year of being really disconnected. It was hard to get going.

My biggest insight is that friendships don't happen if you don't put effort into them. Everyone is busy or in their own routine, so if you want friends, you've gotta focus on it and make an effort. My best social tip is to think about nurturing relationships and then work on them! Work on being thoughtful and fun so that you are the friend that you want other people to be.

I think that when you do that, you win in two ways. For me, I win because I genuinely like being thoughtful to people and building relationships. It makes me feel good as a person and it gets me out of being too self-absorbed—you know, the "me me me" preoccupation. The other way I win is that some of my efforts lead to friendships I really like and enjoy.

Now that I'm in college, I'm making new friends all over again. I still stay connected to friends I made in high school through group texts and Snapchat and by calling them when I can. I think knowing how to make friends is an important skill that I'll use my whole life, especially in big life transitions.

Figuring It Out

We all have social strengths and weaknesses. Skye's natural strength since childhood has been to put care into her friendships. After a time of social disconnection in high school, she reactivated her social superpower and began to again focus on being a good friend in order to create good friends.

Skye used two strategies to get her back in the social game:

1. She focused on putting energy into people around her.

2. She focused on reconnecting with people she'd lost touch with—people she occasionally thought about and missed.

How You Can Use These Strategies

Let's get you comfortable with both of these strategies. Once you're more familiar with them, you can try them, too.

Strategy 1: Start with People Around You

A great way to start nurturing relationships is to look around you. For most teens, school is the biggest regular social setting where they spend time around others their age. Some have different or multiple settings where they are around other teens. For example, you may be around other teens in a youth group, a club, a sport, or some other activity.

Try This: Identify Your Social Settings

To get traction with this strategy, make a list of your social settings. You may have one heading: school. Or you may have more than one: school, soccer, tutoring club.

Now write down as many names as possible of teens associated with each setting. Writing down names is important because it gets you in the habit of truly considering the teens around you as people you can get to know better.

Now review your list of names. Do some people appeal to you more than others? What connections are you willing to put some energy into? Circle those names and warm yourself up to the idea that you can make more of an effort to nurture those connections.

Generate Goals to Move Forward

Now that you have some teens in mind, think of ways you can nurture those connections. Here are some ideas Skye came up with—and they worked!

- Goal 1: Talk to Adrienne in bio. Since we have vocab quizzes every week, I can ask her if she wants to study together. Maybe we can make a routine of it and I can get to know her better.

- Goal 2: Approach Sofia in P. E. and get to know her. I can ask her to be my partner in one of the warm-ups. I can work on letting my personality out more instead of just making it through class keeping to myself.

- Goal 3: Talk more to Emme during lunch. We kind of know each other, but I haven't made much of an effort. I'm going to show more interest in her and extend our conversations beyond the surface. She's in the school play, so maybe I'll ask her more about it and even go to the play.

Your Turn: What Goals Can You Make for Yourself?

Using Skye for inspiration, write down three goals on a piece of paper or in your tips notebook. Energize all three in the next week. Keep creating goals and see what develops.

Just like watering seeds, not all will sprout—and that's okay. Some will and that's what you're going for.

Strategy 2: Communicate and Reconnect

Skye's second strategy was to reconnect with friends with whom she'd lost touch. It is very natural and common for teen girls to go in and out of friendships over the years. You may have "outgrown" some friends or parted ways with them because of a conflict. Sometimes disconnection is a good thing for you because when a relationship doesn't feel healthy, safe, or mutually respectful, it's best to let the person go.

Sometimes, however, disconnection is temporary. In some cases, girls don't even remember what happened to create distance; in other cases, whatever happened doesn't feel that important anymore. Time often heals wounds, which means that a connection that stops working at one point in your life might work beautifully again at another.

It's natural to resist reconnecting because you think it would be "too weird" or you fear your efforts may be rejected. That is a possibility. Sometimes efforts to reconnect don't go the way you'd like because the other person is not responsive. In that case, you might feel hurt and disappointed. But at least you'll know you tried.

A lot of times, however, the other person responds well and a friendship is brought back to life in a new and different way. Because you both are older, you not only get to reclaim your old connection, but you also nurture a new and improved relationship.

In Skye's case, she decided she could handle it if her efforts to reconnect didn't work out. She had already gone through social disappointments and knew through life experience that although disappointment hurts, it could be survived and put in proper perspective.

She also decided the easiest way to reconnect would be to text a few friends she really missed so that she felt less vulnerable about taking the risk. In her communications, Skye apologized for being out of touch. She warmly acknowledged that she missed each person and was thinking about her, hoping she was well.

Since many people respond positively to warm, genuine social effort, Skye did very well with her efforts to reconnect. One friend she messaged did not respond. Skye felt disappointed but decided to trust that it was for the best. Maybe things would change in the future or maybe they wouldn't— she decided she could accept that.

The other three friends responded to her communication, and they successfully reconnected. Over time, Skye's reclaimed friendships became close again. Skye shares, "All three friends told me separately that they'd thought of me, too, but were unsure what to do. They were glad I made the effort to make the first move. I'm happy I did!"

Skye's social bravery and efforts to use these two strategies opened up her social life in a way that felt really good to her—and to her new and reclaimed friends.

Try This: Activate Reconnection

Now, on a piece of paper or in your tips notebook, create a list of friends with whom you've lost touch. Only list people you miss and who you trust can be healthy and positive people in your life. Take some time to reflect on good memories and what you liked about your time together. Now that you've identified possibilities for reconnection, set three goals.

Like Skye, you may want to text an old friend as a way of reaching out. Or maybe you prefer to approach someone on your list in person, with a phone call, or on social media. Whatever you choose, write down the name of the person and your goal for reaching out. Never underestimate the power of friendly, kind communication. Give yourself a week to execute your goals, and be sure to build on the reconnection you activate by nurturing those reconnections to see what blossoms.

More Tips for Nurturing Connections

Now that you've got some possibilities to work with, you can have fun engaging new skills that bring your connections (and reconnections) to life. These skills include checking in with your friends, being a good listener, and bringing fun and light into your relationships. Another important friendship skill is appropriate sharing. Let's take a quick look at each of these skills and hear some tips from teens who have been successful at nurturing friendships.

Check In with Friends

Checking in with friends by asking about their lives and what's important to them shows you care. It's a simple yet powerful way to deepen connection.

Bridget: It bugs me when I have something big going on in my life and my friends don't ask about it. I try to pay attention to what's going on with my friends and show I care by checking in with them.

For example, my friend Eva got her wisdom teeth out, so I remembered that and made sure to visit her and text her. She really appreciated it because a lot of her friends completely forgot. If I were the one stuck on the couch with a puffy face and a lot of pain, I wouldn't want to feel forgotten. That's what motivates me to take the time and effort to check in.

Your Turn: Check In with Yourself— About Checking In with Others

How are you at remembering what's going on in the lives of your friends and checking in with them? Check in with yourself and see if this is something you could improve on.

How to Improve Check-Ins:

- **Pay attention** when someone says something about herself or her life that seems important. For example: If Devon's dad just moved out or Mattea's kitty is missing, make a mental note of that as something more important than the daily chitchat. And then *remember* to check in with them about it.

- **Offer support.** Your friend might want and need help, and your willingness to *ask* shows you care. For example: "I'm sorry. Do you want to talk about it?" or "Let's put signs up about your cat and I'll help you look."

- **Write a reminder.** You carry a lot of information in your brain and it's easy to forget a friend has an important date coming up. For example: Ashleigh tells you she has a big dance performance next week. Write a reminder for yourself on a sticky note and place it somewhere obvious, or create a reminder on your phone.

Listen with Your Heart: Being a Good Listener

Good listeners are often valued friends. They have the ability to communicate interest, respect, compassion, understanding, and support. A good talker who is also a good listener, Alexi says she pays attention to what friends share so they know they are important to her.

Alexi: I'm a good listener because I don't interrupt and I don't change the subject back to me if I'm listening to a friend that really needs my full attention.

My parents taught me to listen with my heart, which means I get into the state of really caring about the person I'm listening to. I don't let my phone distract me either, because I get annoyed when people do that to me when I'm talking.

There are other things that make me a good listener, like staying on topic and asking questions and stuff like that, but mainly I just really pay attention and make what other people are saying important to me.

Your Turn: Good Listeners

Listening is an important skill. Think of someone you know who is a very good listener. How does that person make you feel when you are talking? Now think of someone who is not a good listener. How does that person make you feel? If you like, note your thoughts on a piece of paper or in your tips notebook.

Tips for Better Listening

* **Make eye contact.** Really. You'll notice good listeners tend to make eye contact, nod, and give signs that they are listening, like "Yeah," "Uh huh," and so on.

* **Relax your body.** When you intentionally relax the muscles of your body, you tap into a more present and receptive listening mindset. You're more likely to truly connect to what the other person is saying, and you're less likely to interrupt.

* **Put yourself in the shoes of the person talking.** Imagine what you would think and feel if you were in the other person's shoes. When you do this, you

are practicing empathy. People who are empathic tend to be very good at forming and sustaining close relationships.

* **Focus on what's important**. Good listeners can tell when they need to really pay attention. A lot of teen talk is fun and "filler," but sometimes it's not. In those more important moments, good listeners focus with love and attention. If a friend mentions something that sounds significant, let her know you care by going back to what she said and gently asking more about it.

Lighten Up

Most people really appreciate being with someone who has a good sense of humor. People who can see the light side of life are fun and put things in perspective. They often communicate an energy of friendliness that serves as a magnet for other people because good energy is contagious. Here's Ruby's suggestion for "lightening up":

Ruby: I'm a fun person. I like to laugh and make other people laugh. I don't mind getting deep with my friends and going through hard times, but, honestly, nothing bonds people together better than a good laugh and a fun time.

My friends like my sense of humor a lot because it helps us all keep a grip on the big picture—we are kids and life is supposed to be fun.

How is your sense of humor and fun? If you tend to be serious, would you like to be more lighthearted and playful? While not everyone is a comedian, you can remind yourself to be playful, have fun, and lighten up. Try to see the bright side of life or be willing to break stress and tension with silliness and humor. As Ruby points out, a lot of bonding happens when girls are sharing laughs and good times.

Your Turn: Lightening Up

Take a few moments to think about how you approach life. If you're often serious, how could you "lighten up" a bit? If you hide your sense of humor, how can you share it with others more easily? How could having fun with your friends nurture your connections? Write your thoughts on a piece of paper or in your tips notebook.

Tips for Fun with Friends

* **Be a kid again.** Get water balloons on a hot day, get out the sidewalk chalk and create a work of art, or play dress-up.

* **Be playful.** Look for funny opportunities around you. Be silly or even ridiculous at times, crack a fun-loving joke—but *never* at the expense of others. (Teen girls often play off their hurt feelings in the moment but agonize over the jab later.)

* **Give fun away.** Make small gifts for others, such as cookies, bracelets, and art. Don't be afraid to be ridiculous. If you made daisy chains, pinch pots, or

origami when you were little, make them again and give them as gifts to friends.

* **Plan fun stuff.** Create lists with your friends of fun stuff to do. Spending quality time with friends makes you closer. Also, when friends do things together, they tend to think of and plan more things to do together in the future.

Letting People In: Appropriate and Inappropriate Sharing

Letting people in by opening up is a big way that people get close. It is equally true that skill and awareness are involved in healthy sharing. While some girls struggle with opening up even a little bit, other girls may open up too much and share too much, too soon, and with the wrong people.

When you feel a foundation of interest and trust in a friendship, sharing feels good for both people. Zoe has more to say on sharing and oversharing:

Zoe: I've learned that letting people into your private life creates closeness. Healthy sharing is when you get to know someone one step at a time, and the process of revealing personal info unfolds in a way that feels good to the sharer and also the listener. When you decide to share more of yourself, I think it's a good idea to decide what you're okay with sharing so that you feel you're balancing your desire to get closer with your need to feel emotionally safe and comfortable.

Oversharing happens when a person allows personal information to tumble out without checking in with herself—without considering how the other person will be affected by what she's sharing. Oversharing is more reckless, and I think it's less healthy and can even strain a relationship instead of building closeness. People who overshare make me uncomfortable, and instead of feeling special and trusted, I feel stressed. I think oversharing leaves the sharer overexposed and the listener overwhelmed!

Teens who have learned the difference between "sharing" and "oversharing" offer examples of how they've created closer friendships by letting people in:

Aisha: Sometime when people are planning on getting alcohol and drinking and they want to know why I don't want to drink, I let them know I have a history of addiction in my family. I don't give too many details unless it's someone I really know and that person's interested. But sharing this has helped people know me and understand me better, and people definitely respect me for being honest.

Elle: I have issues with test anxiety and I used to keep it a secret. Then one of my friends told me she gets test anxiety really bad, and so I told her I do, too. It made us closer. Now we try to support each other with it.

Julia: Most people assume that I'm really confident because I give that impression. I do very well in school and people assume I'm really smart because of my grades. They also think that school is easy for me. I think it made some of my friends uncomfortable and maybe intimidated them until I shared with them that I work extremely hard, and I'm terrified of doing poorly and getting anything lower than an A. When I shared this, I became more human to them.

When I let them in, it made us closer and I feel better now that they know the real story and not just how things appear from the outside. They even help me keep perspective with my grade obsession by saying sweet things that help me know that they would feel the same about me no matter what grades I got.

Your Turn: Getting Sharing Just Right

How about you? Do you let people in too little, too much, or—baby bear style—just right?

When girls don't share about themselves at all, think or write (on a piece of paper or in your tips notebook) about how that affects you and your sense of closeness with them. When girls overshare, how does that affect you and your sense of how connected you want to be with them?

Try This: Appropriate Sharing or Oversharing

Appropriate sharing brings girls closer. Oversharing is potentially unsafe for the girl who is sharing because others may not understand or keep her confidence. Oversharing also puts other girls in an awkward position because they don't necessarily want the burden of TMI—too much information!

Check out the following examples and guess which describe appropriate sharing—something that will bring girls closer—and which describe oversharing: too much information that makes everyone uncomfortable.

Appropriate Sharing or Oversharing

- Val shares with the volleyball team that she just came from her psychiatry appointment, that she's been diagnosed with depression, and that she was prescribed an antidepressant. Most of the girls look at her blankly.

- Melody shares with her friend Emily that she's been feeling out of shape and bad about herself. The girls begin talking about body image and how to support each other in healthy ways.

- Angel mentions to a classmate sitting next to her in geometry that she is completely confused about the chapter. The classmate offers to help her during break, and the two become study buddies and eventually friends.

- Cali asks Hannah why they never hang out at Hannah's house. Hannah confides that her older brother has issues and is unpredictable to be around. Cali gives a warm and reassuring response and the two girls feel closer to each other.

You probably figured out that the first example involving Val's disclosure is oversharing, and the other examples are appropriate sharing. In Val's case, the information she shared was much too personal for that situation. It is likely she would have received a more supportive response if she had privately discussed her appointment with her best friend away from the volleyball team. The conversation would have been confidential, and because Val's friend knows her, she might have understood where Val was coming from in ways the team probably didn't.

Your Turn: Your Sharing Style

How about you? Think about yourself and your life. What might you appropriately share with a trusted friend? What feels too personal or private to share?

Always take care of yourself by honoring your own need for privacy when it comes to highly personal information about yourself or aspects of your life. Some girls find that when they are bothered by something too personal to share with a friend, it helps to journal about it or to talk to a safe adult like a teacher, counselor, or family member.

The Next Step: Guarding Against Threats

In this chapter, you've learned ways you can become a better friend and deepen the quality of both your new and old relationships. Now it's time to guard against threats to the friendships you have been nurturing. These threats are very common and show up in many groups of people, including teenage girls. Like weeds in your garden, once you know they're there, you can figure out how to "weed" them out. Turn to the next chapter, Tip 5: Weed Out Negative Social Habits, to learn how to enhance your "weeding" skills.

Just-For-Fun Quiz: On a Trip to the Zoo, Which One Are You?

Are you a lion, a dolphin, or a monkey? Find out which animal you are and get tips for social growth. Select the answer that best fits you and write it on a piece of paper or in your tips notebook.

1. If you could go on a vacation tomorrow, you would go

    A. camping or to a cabin with your family.

    B. to a big city with a few of your favorite people.

    C. traveling with your closest friend.

2. Your favorite thing to do on the weekend is

    A. hang out with a friend.

    B. chill around your house.

    C. go somewhere where there are lots of people, preferably with several friends.

3. When you need to talk, you turn to

    A. one friend in particular.

    B. a member of your family.

    C. a group of friends that you share everything with.

4. You spend most of your money on

    A. group activities and outings.

    B. presents for birthdays and holidays.

    C. getting a bite with a friend or going to the movies.

5. You most enjoy

    A. an overnight with a friend, staying up late and talking.

    B. sleeping in your own bed, in your own home.

    C. a house party where a group of girls stay and spend the night.

SCORING

Add up your points.

1. A = 1 B = 3 C = 2

2. A = 2 B = 1 C = 3

3. A = 2 B =1 C = 3

4. A = 3 B = 1 C = 2

5. A = 2 B = 1 C = 3

1–5 points: You are a lion.

The lion is a family animal. As a lion, you are close with your family and often pass on hanging out with others. When you are social away from family, you look forward to being home again to decompress. A great way for you to increase social contact is to chat with kids in class and join clubs or activities that create a sense of social family for you. You can also invite new friends to join your family's get-togethers. As a lion, you are great at working with other people. Challenge yourself to create new social families that enrich your life and build your social confidence.

6–10 points: You are a dolphin.

Dolphins are social creatures that have fun together and enjoy companionship. They enjoy socializing, but tend to stick with who they know, showing great affection for their "familiars." They also enjoy activities that they've done before, and are therefore comfortable with. As a dolphin, you can challenge yourself to meet more friends of your friends. Let your established friends know that new people are invited and welcome next time you go to the movies, to lunch, or just out and about. Enjoy your established friends, but at the same time, seek to widen the circle of people you include in your plans and activities.

11–15 points: You are a monkey.

Monkeys are very social animals. As a monkey, you tend to like being around other people and you have a lot of social energy. Being with friends may be your favorite way to spend time, and you may even feel like you already have plenty of social contact. The best way for you to grow socially is to establish a deeper level of friendship with one or two people you already know. You can do that by being a great listener, making more time for deep talks, and asking questions that are a little more personal. You may also share something that is a little more personal to encourage more intimate connection. In doing this, you will have both quality and quantity of social connection.

tip 5

Weed Out Negative Social Habits

So far, you are learning tips that will help you blossom into a more confident and outgoing person. Keep working on all your new skills and repeat them so often that they become your new *positive* social habits. A habit, after all, is a behavior that you repeat so often that it becomes part of your routine—part of who you are and the way you live your life.

Positive habits are awesome because they make you feel good and they get you where you want to go. Just as positive study habits lead to improved learning and doing well in school, positive social habits lead to feeling good and connecting well with other people.

Of course, not all habits are positive. Sometimes negative habits pop up like weeds and are tough to get rid of. They sneak into your everyday life and get in the way of your goals and your ability to feel good about yourself. This chapter is about identifying negative social habits so you can weed them right out of your social garden.

Even the sweetest girls can have negative social habits; all good people can have some bad habits. So, it's time to grab your gardening tools and get those weeds out of there!

Common Negative Social Habits

Ever heard or said anything like this?

* "Did you see Maggie's booty shorts? I wonder if she knows her entire butt is hanging out."

* "Guys just like her 'cause she'll hook up with anyone."

* "That girl is such a bitch. I've heard nothing but bad things about her."

* "Shelley broke up with Ryan and already hooked up with someone else at a party over the weekend."

* "She's pretty I guess, but I hear she's not the smartest..."

Ever thought anything like this?

* *I would never ask Nadia if she wants to go to lunch. She wouldn't want to.*

* *Even though I miss hanging out with Dana, I still avoid her. I feel like we're too different now and it wouldn't be the same.*

* *I can tell they are talking shit about me whenever I walk by.*

* *I want to text Aubrey to see how she is, but she's obsessed with her relationship. I don't think I should.*

* *I want to go to the game tonight, but I don't think anyone wants to go with me.*

The lists above depict examples of common negative social habits you're going to learn more about. In the first set of statements, girls are *judging* other girls—and then sharing those judgments with others, which means they are also *gossiping*. In the second set, girls are *making assumptions* about others that may not even be true. As you learn more about these common negative habits, they will be easier for you to identify, understand, and get under control.

Miranda, a social gardening pro, tells her story about how taming her own negative social habits changed her social life for the better. She's eager to share her thoughts with you because she feels that if she knew in high school what she knows now, she could have had a more interesting assortment of high school friends—and a whole lot more fun.

✳ *Meet Miranda, Age 19*

The quote that inspires her:

> *I don't like that man. I must get to know him better.*
> —Abraham Lincoln

Miranda is a college freshman who, inspired by Lincoln's quote, has a lot to say about weeding bad habits out of her social garden.

I used to make judgments and assumptions about girls and let my opinions determine how I felt and acted toward them. I would judge girls as slutty, stuck up, shallow, bitchy, dumb—along those lines. And even though I didn't think of myself as critical, I allowed my opinions to affect me a lot.

As I got older, I just stopped that behavior, because I learned that my judgments and assumptions about people were often wrong. I took a class in Women's Studies my first year in college, and the class helped me realize I don't want to be negative toward other women. We should support one another and accept each other—not judge and have unnecessary drama just because of the "differences" we think we have.

This is my tip: Keep an open mind about everyone— people have different sides to them. And everyone has a "back story," so you really can't judge with any accuracy unless you really, really know the person and her entire context.

Some of my best friends in college are people I would have judged when I was younger. Or I would have assumed they were too different from me to be my friends. As you get older, you realize people who may be very different from you can add a lot to your social life and to your richness as a person.

Now I think of judgments and assumptions as weeds to root out of my thinking habits. I've gotta say, my social life is more diverse and interesting because of it.

Figuring It Out

Miranda realized that making judgments and assumptions kept her from being friends with people she actually may have liked. As she got older and wiser, she realized many of her negative social habits were based on ideas that weren't even accurate.

When Miranda was a younger teen, she never questioned her judgments or assumptions. She accepted everything she thought as true. When she began taking a closer look at her judgments and assumptions and how they affected her social life, she could see that many of her conclusions about people were inaccurate and that these inaccurate thoughts actually controlled her behavior and limited her.

When Miranda realized this, she began to identify her judgments and assumptions and question them. For example, she formed an opinion that a girl in her class was so stuck-up (judgment) that she wouldn't like Miranda (assumption). Once Miranda began questioning her judgments and assumptions, she got to know the girl better and found that the girl responded to Miranda's efforts to be friendly, and opened the door for many new friends as well. Gradually, Miranda started pushing past her negative opinions so that she could get to know people and then get a sense of what was true and what wasn't. Let's take a closer look at the habits Miranda chose to work on.

Weed Out Judgments and Assumptions

When you make a judgment about a girl, you place a critical label on her based on your impression, gossip, or limited information. Slut, stuck-up, and bitch are common labels girls place on other girls.

Try This: Discovering Your Judgments and Assumptions

Using a piece of paper or your tips notebook, make two columns. At the top of column 1, write "Judgment"; at the top of column 2, write "Based On…" Write down as many of your judgments as you can think of, along with what they are based on. Keep your work close by because you will soon add to it. These examples may help you get started:

Judgment	Based On...
Bayley is stuck up.	She's a cheerleader.
Karli doesn't like me.	She doesn't smile when she looks at me.
Kim is a bitch.	She has a bitchy look on her face and isn't friendly.

When you make an assumption about someone, you have an idea, opinion, or belief that you accept as true without any proof. For example, these four common assumptions may affect you and your social life:

- You don't like someone.

- Another person won't like you or doesn't like you.

- Someone is above or below you.

- You assume what you've heard about someone is true and let your assumption affect the way you think about her and act toward her.

Now, make two more columns on your piece of paper or in your tips notebook. At the top of column 1, write "Assumptions"; at the top of column 2, write "Based on..." Think about the assumptions you make and write down as many as possible and what they're based on. Here are some examples to get you started:

Assumption	Based On...
Bailey would never like me	We're too different; I'm not in her group of friends.
Even though Kim is struggling in algebra, too, she would never want to study together. If I asked her, she could be bitchy to me.	I tend to believe what people say, I guess.

Your Turn: Cultivating a Positive Social Habit

In the previous exercise, you identified some of your judgments and assumptions. Now take a few quiet moments and reflect on the questions below. You may want to write your answers on a piece of paper or in your tips notebook.

- Do my judgments and assumptions hold me back from being friendly and respectful?

- Do my judgments and assumptions hold me back from keeping an open mind and figuring out for myself how I feel about a particular person?

- What if my judgments and assumptions are wrong and keep me from even a small connection with someone? (For example, you and Kim might not be best pals, but you could still support one another in algebra.)

Remembering to question your judgments and assumptions by asking yourself these questions is a positive social habit. You may catch yourself in a negative habit and then decide to weed it out of your life.

If you're in the mood, think of small ways you can adjust your behavior so that judgments and assumptions no longer limit you. For example, "I'm going to ask Kim if she wants to study for the test after school with me. I'll decide for myself what she's like." Write your thoughts on a piece of paper or in your tips notebook.

Reality Check

Sometimes negative judgments and assumptions are true; sometimes they are a little bit true, and sometimes they are completely false. More often than you'd guess, they are false and based on incomplete or misunderstood information.

No matter what the case is, as Miranda noted above, there is probably more to the story than you know. Usually, what other people do makes perfect sense when you have more information about their unique history and circumstances. In other words, if you walked a mile in another girl's flip-flops, you would see that how she thinks/dresses/acts/lives her life makes sense, even if you wouldn't think/dress/act/live your life exactly the same way.

Of course, you don't have to be besties with anyone you don't like or whose values are vastly different from yours. You can, however, be nonjudgmental, friendly, and respectful to everyone, no matter what.

Open Hearts and Minds

The positive habit of keeping an open heart and mind toward everyone may not seem like a crucial component to social success, but it is! It's also part of your true nature—meaning the person you truly are, before you took on negative habits. As a child, for example, even if you were shy, you likely had an open, nonjudgmental attitude toward all kinds of people, no matter how they looked or how they were "categorized" by others.

Girls who have open hearts and minds find that they attract good experiences and people who share the same positive social qualities. Open-minded, open-hearted people attract other open-minded, open-hearted people, just as we are drawn toward a warm fire on a cold night.

When you put out positive energy everywhere you go, your life warms up and positive energy comes back to you. Of course, if experience teaches you someone is not emotionally or physi-cally safe for you to have in your life, you want to honor that and step back. Having an open heart and mind does not mean that you allow mistreatment or harm. It means that until you have experience to the contrary, you are open and respectful—even friendly—to as many people as possible.

Progress, Not Perfection

Making progress as you start eliminating negative social habits is very empowering. However, it would be unrealistic to expect to completely eliminate all judgments and assumptions. It's human nature to form ideas and opinions by labeling the world around us. Your mission is to notice and question your judgments, not to eliminate them entirely.

Remind yourself that some judgments are based on real information, such as "she's in the school play." Others are based on superficial impressions or little information, such as "she's stuck-up because she's in the school play."

You don't like it when other people form superficial judg-ments about you, so check yourself to make sure you are not making superficial judgments about others. Be willing to notice and question your habits so you can determine which are help-ing and which are hurting your social life.

Here's how Miranda did it: "I just developed a habit of real-izing when I'm making snap judgments and assumptions. Then I ask myself, *Wait, what if this isn't true? How would I be acting right now if I didn't believe this opinion I'm creating that's based on basically nothing?*"

Learning from Miranda's experiences will be a big social advantage, but don't think you're done with weeding out bad habits yet. There's a doozy of a weed we still have not dealt with. It's time to...

Weed Out Gossip

Gossip is talking about other people in a negative way, behind their backs. Often gossip takes over positive communication, just as weeds can take over a garden, choking off the growth of desirable plants. Gossip can also take the place of positive interactions and become negative and hurtful; it can spring up everywhere and be hard to get rid of. A reluctant expert on the subject, Megan, learned more about the weeds of gossip than she wanted to know.

✱ *Meet Megan, Age 16*

Quotes that inspire her:

> *Strong minds discuss ideas, average minds discuss events, weak minds discuss people.* —Socrates

> *Whatever words we utter should be chosen with care for people will hear them and be influenced by them for good or ill.* —Attributed to Buddha

Megan was very inspired by these quotes. She says:

I chose these quotes because they all work together. Obviously, Socrates and Buddha have great points and those quotes inspire me.

At the same time, the reality is that teen girls are going to talk about each other. We can't help being interested in each other, and I guess the dark side of that interest is to get negative and hurtful when we talk. That's what gossip is, right? So this is my tip: Watch out for gossip! It was a big issue for me this year.

It started one day when I was talking to some of my friends about my frustrations with another friend that I had on-and-off problems with. I was under the impression that everyone in my group agreed with what I was saying and shared my frustrations. But I guess I wasn't just "talking" about my friend. What I was really doing was talking shit about her—and she found out about it.

It was a huge drama. First, she acted weird with me and excluded me from some social things. Then she confronted me and had very specific details about the things I was saying. Awkward.

I realized the "private" conversations I was having with my other friends, who I thought were supporting me, were not private. They were talking about me talking about her, and the whole thing blew up so that I was on bad terms with everyone. I felt totally alone and like all of a sudden everyone had a problem with me. It was the worst.

Figuring It Out

Though Megan learned that gossiping can blow up in a very disruptive way, the truth is that just about everyone does it. Check out this list of reasons why girls gossip and make a mental note of which ones you can relate to:

* To vent their frustration

* Because it can be a relief to focus on someone else

* As a way of connecting to each other

* Because sharing scandal adds excitement to the day

* To discharge feelings of jealousy

* Because criticizing other girls helps them feel better about themselves

Although there's been a lot of media hype about "Mean Girls" and girls are often depicted on reality television shows as heartless and evil, the truth is that few teen girls gossip to intentionally hurt other girls. It can happen, but it's not common.

Usually, the people gossiping are not thinking of the potential harm the gossip can cause. More often, girls are absorbed in the pleasure and relief they get from focusing on other people and are actually emotionally disconnected from the effects the gossip could have on others.

Because teen girls feel so much pressure to be good enough, smart enough, pretty enough, cool enough, athletic enough (and more!), they sometimes focus on negative characteristics of other girls and then discuss or *gossip* about those characteristics.

Your Turn: Your Gossip Habits

Using a piece of paper or your tips notebook, write about the role gossip plays in your life. Take an honest and brave look at yourself and identify any gossiping habits you may want to change.

Here are some prompts you can use:

- Are you are a light gossiper or a heavy one?

- What do you get out of it?

- How hard would it be to break your gossip habit?

- Do you think gossiping less would have a positive effect on the way you feel about yourself as a person?

- What would the impact be on other people?

- Have you ever been hurt by gossip? How did that affect you?

You can use all of those prompts or none of them. Or, instead of writing, you can give yourself a few moments to contemplate your personal answer to the questions above.

Top Tips for Gossip Control

Teen girls offer the following tips for weeding gossip out of your garden. As you read each tip, ask yourself if it might work for you.

Riley: I try to change the subject when gossip gets mean, and sometimes I try to say something good about the person who is getting talked about. It works a lot of the time because my friends will kinda stop and hear themselves and how negative they sound, and then we change the direction of the conversation.

Sabrina: I find that I am the person who starts gossip! I have learned to catch myself and say, "Ahhhh! Wait! I'm talking shit again." My friends laugh and we change the topic.

Gina: I've had a huge problem gossiping. I don't mean to be negative, but I'm just interested in social drama and it's hard to not talk about it. So I try to walk a line where I don't say anything that terrible about anyone…but I will talk about what's going on with them. That's still not *good*, but it's an improvement for me. I'm just going for improvement, and as I get older, the gossip is dying down a little with all my friends. I think we have more perspective that it's not cool and maybe more self-control to just not go there like we did constantly when we were freshmen.

Jessie: I will literally go mute when gossip gets bad. I find some reason to leave the situation.

Shelby: When I'm tempted to gossip, I try to imagine that the gossip will definitely get back to the person I'm talking about. It kind of ruins the fun for me because I've been that girl who people are talking about, and it hurts.

Alisha: My rule is that I *never* say anything bad about anyone's appearance. I think it's low and it's a line I won't cross. Most of my friends know this about me.

Lead the Way

As you can see from these tips, improving your own behavior is a good strategy for pulling some weedy gossip out of your garden. Try the following experiments and see how they work for you:

* **Don't gossip for a day.** Yep, give yourself an assignment to abstain from gossip for an entire day. If you're around other people that day, you might be surprised to see how challenging this is.

* **Take a stand.** Say something to your friends about gossip: "Hey, we are gossiping, you guys. Let's stop." It's simple and gets the point across.

* **Offer a positive perspective**. When gossip starts flowing, you can slow it down by offering a perspective such as, "Hey, you guys, we don't know if any of this is really true and we wouldn't want other people talking about us and our lives this way" or "There are things we don't know about this, you guys, so we should just stay out of it."

Your Turn: Being Part of the Solution

If you're motivated, try each of the previous suggestions and write about it on a piece of paper or in your tips notebook. Give yourself a lot of credit for being part of the gossiping solution.

Megan learned the hard way that it is easier to nurture and protect friendships than to repair them once they are broken. Now, when she's tempted to gossip, she reminds herself of that and finds that this helps her have the courage to opt out or change the subject.

Moving On

Now that you've seen the importance of weeding out negative social habits before they threaten your relationships, you will learn how to use communication to solve other problems when they come up. In the next chapter, Tip 6: Communicate Through Conflict, you'll even get an update on Megan as she shares how she learned to use better skills through a time of great social conflict.

Just-For-Fun Quiz: Identify Your Internal Support System

On a piece of paper or in your tips notebook, indicate whether each statement is true or false.

1. When I have a zit or am having a bad hair day, I try to remind myself that it's no big deal.

2. When I take a risk that I know is necessary or will be good for me, I think of all the things that could go wrong.

3. When I'm nervous about something, I try to talk myself through it.

4. In general, I expect people to either like me or feel neutral toward me.

5. When I'm nervous about a new situation, I fake it 'til I make it because that's a great strategy.

6. When I finish a project, I tend to think I could have done better.

7. I try to pump myself up before I do something that intimidates me.

8. I seem to get more confident by doing things that make me nervous, because when I get through them, I feel proud of myself.

9.   I tend to judge myself and other people harshly.

10. I get really mad at myself when I make a mistake.

11. When something goes poorly in my life, I try to learn from it and then move on.

SCORING

Next to your answers on the paper or in your tips notebook, write "I" or "C" based on the list below. For example, if you answered false to question 1, write "I" for inner critic next to your answer; if you answered true, write "C" for cheerleader.

	Inner Critic	Cheerleader
1.	False	True
2.	True	False
3.	False	True
4.	False	True
5.	False	True
6.	True	False
7.	True	False
8.	False	True
9.	True	False
10.	True	False
11.	False	True

This will tell you what kind of Internal Support System you have.

What's an internal support system? Your internal support system refers to the way you either support yourself—or get down on yourself—in your head. The more supportive you are toward yourself in your thoughts and attitude, the more easily you will be able to nudge yourself forward in life. Supporting yourself enables you to take beneficial risks by leaving your comfort zone.

Inner Critic: If you listed more "I" responses than "C" responses, you have an inner critic in your head who tends to be hard on you. It may feel like this inner critic helps you, but it really doesn't! Everyone does better with positive encouragement, especially when they are working on making positive changes in themselves and in their lives. *Take Note*: Your inner critic may be holding you back. Try to notice the thoughts your inner critic sends you so that you can work with them instead of feeling crushed by them. Work on cultivating a kinder inner voice, like the cheerleader!

Cheerleader: If you listed more "C" responses than "I" responses, you have an inner cheerleader who cheers you on with positive thinking, encouragement, and reassurance. You tend to get through tough times by listening to your cheerleader and moving forward. You don't expect perfection from yourself or other people, and your strategy under stress is to think good thoughts, hope for the best, and keep moving forward. *Take Note*: This ability to be positive is great for you and other people. Keep it up and share it with others!

tip 6

Communicate Through Conflict

Do you cringe at the thought of having conflict with others? If you're hurt or angry because of someone else's behavior, are you more likely to deny your feelings, let them fester quietly, or talk to other girls instead of confronting the girl with whom you have the issue? If your answer to any of these questions is yes, you are 100 percent completely normal. People of all ages stress out when it comes to communicating through conflict. With big feelings and an enormous preference for keeping your social life drama-free, why wouldn't you deny, fester, or avoid? Unfortunately, those options don't always work and often create even more tension in relationships.

Since this survival guide is about building your social skills so that you can handle good times as well as challenging times with friends, Tip 6 will help you face your fear of conflict with other girls and actually work through conflicts to make your relationships stronger. Yep, that can happen!

Communication skills to use in times of conflict are crucial because they will help you feel confident in handling challenges with friends. Dealing with issues directly and skillfully helps you strengthen friendships before bad feelings create damage. By the time you're finished with this chapter, you will be able to protect your friendships from falling apart during times of conflict. Taylor's story is a great example of how important communicating through conflict can be.

✳ *Meet Taylor, Age 18*

The quote that inspires her:

> *My belief is that communication is the best way to create strong relationships.* —Jada Pinkett Smith

I come from a communicative family, I'd say. We talk to each other a lot, and because there are three girls in my family, we don't hold anything back when we're upset with each other. If my little sister does something that I feel is disrespectful to me, I'm gonna let her know. If my older sister is acting like she's my mom, I'm gonna tactfully call her out on it.

It's not like we're savage or anything—we're just direct. And usually skillful, because my mom says you can say anything you need to say if you take the time to say it skillfully—not abusively.

My parents say it's normal to have conflict. The important thing is to communicate directly and respectfully, listen patiently, and work through it.

My friends call me the therapist of our grade, but trust me, I know nothing about being a therapist. I just know how to express myself no matter what I'm feeling, and some of my friends have trouble with that. They think it's going to cause drama or break up a friendship if they tell someone they're hurt over something or angry about something.

My belief is that if you don't talk about it, bad feelings damage or even end the friendship—or the girls involved start talking to other people and that makes everything dramatic and bad. Why would anybody think talking to everyone except the girl involved is a good idea? I think that is a misguided attempt to minimize drama that blows up. You might as well go directly to the source.

I help my friends by supporting them to go to the person they are upset with, say what they need to say in the best way possible, and move on. Girls are afraid that speaking up will cause problems, but I think the opposite is true: burying feelings is what causes problems. My advice to girls is to trust that they can be direct and communicative, even in times of conflict. It's better to put issues on the table than to stuff them down. Trust yourself and trust other girls to be able to talk through feelings and problems. It just might turn out that you're even better friends because of it.

Figuring It Out

Taylor is not afraid of conflict because she was taught growing up that it's normal and not something terrible to be avoided. Because she knows the importance of addressing social conflicts when they arise, she's come up with a three-step communication strategy that has worked well for her, and will also work well for you. You will learn her strategy in a minute. First, check out this dialogue between two five-year-old girls. Enjoy it and make mental notes, because the beautiful simplicity of kindergartners will guide you toward better communication in your own life.

Claire: Laurel, you said we were gonna jump rope at recess, but you forgot me and I'm sad and mad. I wanna jump rope with you still. Can you get off the monkey bars now?

Laurel: I'm sorry, Claire. I forgot. Let's go now! The bell hasn't rung yet.

Cute, funny, or genius? Taylor says:

All three, of course, and this is what I do, only with a little less bluntness. I try to put the issue into words that aren't blaming or super confrontational, and then I talk about my feelings and offer an idea or solution. That's it. I won't say it's easy 100 percent of the time, but if you have a basic idea of the points you want to make, you don't have to overthink it and make it a bigger thing than it really is.

Let's organize Taylor's advice into a three-step process.

Three-Step Communication

Here's how kindergartner Claire demonstrates three-step communication:

1. She describes the problem to Laurel.

2. She shares her feelings about the problem.

3. She asks for what she'd like to have happen.

Let's take a closer look at each of these steps.

Step 1: Describe the problem.

In Claire's case, the problem was clear to her. She and Laurel had a plan and Laurel forgot. Without blaming Laurel and saying something harsh—like "I can't believe you blew me off to do monkey bars!"—Claire left blaming and confrontation out and stuck to describing the issue at hand: "You said we were gonna jump rope at recess, but you forgot me."

Your Turn: Identify What Happened

Practice step 1 by using an example of a problem from your own life. On a piece of paper or in your tips notebook, write step 1 and, as simply as you can, describe a problem you have had with someone in your life (friend, relative, acquaintance). You can choose a recent problem or one from your past, a big problem or a tiny one. The point is to practice identifying what happened as if you were an invisible reporter recording what you observe.

Step 2: Share your feelings.

Sometimes life is simple and your feelings are clear to you. For example, "I am nervous about this test" or "I am annoyed with my brother." Other times, however, you may not be sure what you're feeling: "I know I'm uncomfortable around Tiffany, but I don't know why." In Claire's case, her feelings were clear to her and she shared them with Laurel without hesitation: "I'm sad and mad."

Your Turn: Recognize Your Feelings

Practice step 2 by writing down the feelings you experienced as a result of the problem you identified in step 1.

In problem situations, people may feel sad, mad, hurt, angry, jealous, confused, intimidated, shocked, outraged, scared, nervous, terrified, betrayed, hopeless, powerless, and more. Maybe one or more of those feelings fits for you and the situation you are working with. For a larger list of feelings, see the table below.

Table of Feelings

Love	Trust	Hate
Fear	Anticipation	Gratitude
Anger	Surprise	Pride
Sadness	Hurt	Hope
Joy	Confusion	Guilt
Disgust	Envy	Comfort

Try This: How to Identify Your Feelings

As you think about the situation you wrote about in step 1, your feeling or feelings might come to you quickly, as they did for Claire. If your feelings are harder to identify, try this:

- Close your eyes and breathe deeply as you allow yourself to fully access the memory of the problem.

- As you remember, notice what's happening in your body, and you will likely become aware of feelings associated with the memory.

- Invite feelings to come into your awareness, identify them, see if you can label them (for example, sad and mad), then release them.

The more you work to get to know your feelings, the better you will get at labeling them and releasing them. You might notice one feeling (such as hurt) or a combination of several feelings (hurt, anger, jealousy, insecurity). Recognizing your feelings will help you identify your need.

Step 3: Ask for what you'd like to have happen.

In an effort to meet her own need to jump rope with Laurel, Claire articulated what she'd like to have happen: "I wanna jump rope with you still. Can you get off the monkey bars?"

Asking for what you'd like to have happen is an important step that teen girls may forget. You may be tracking other people more than yourself, and while that's thoughtful, your social life will actually be better if you find a balance between being aware of other people's needs and of your own. Step 3 is extremely important because it's hard to create an outcome that you'd like if you don't know what you want and aren't able to communicate it.

Your Turn: Identify What You'd Like to Have Happen

Look again at steps 1 and 2 from your personal scenario. Ask yourself what you would have liked to have happen. At the time, maybe it happened and maybe it did not. The point for you now is to practice identifying and articulating *your need* in that situation. Take a few quiet moments, then on a piece of paper or in your tips notebook, write what your need was in that situation. How could you have asked for what you needed?

Learning to describe the problem, share feelings, and ask for what you need may seem a little hard at first, but as you practice the steps you will find the skills become almost automatic. Next, you will want to decide the best time to use them.

When to Use Three-Step Communication

When you have an issue with someone, the idea of talking about it can be so stressful that you may be tempted to avoid the conversation. If so, a good rule of thumb is that if you are hurt or angry with a friend and the feeling doesn't pass within two days, you will benefit from using the three-step communication strategy to achieve healing and resolution.

Another great benefit of three-step communication is that instead of feeling a knot of thoughts, feelings, and needs when you're upset with someone, you will be able to separate thoughts (what happened) from your feelings (hurt, anger), and then identify what you'd like to have happen (desired outcome). The separation of these three communication components allows you to feel clear inside and communicate clearly on the outside. (That's much better than being stuck with the "knot" inside your stomach that throbs painfully—or turns into hot lava that eventually erupts out of your mouth and melts your relationship.)

As you become experienced and confident at communicating to resolve social conflict, you might find yourself communicating upset feelings on the spot or as soon you perceive there's a problem. When you know you can say things in a skillful way and often get good results, why not take care of business right away? Here's an example:

Luna: Hey Cali, I can't hang out after school today. Jake's gotta do something for his dad and I said I'd go with him.

Cali: Okay, Luna, but I'm just upset that you've broken after-school plans with me three times now to hang out with Jake. It's a little irritating to me, so next time we make plans, please make sure you can keep them.

Luna: Wow, I wasn't aware at all. Okay, Cali, sorry. I will work on that.

That exchange between Luna and Cali was clear and direct. Cali did a great job with three-step communication and Luna did a great job hearing the feedback without getting prickly and defensive. Hearing feedback like that in a mature and accountable way is more important in a friendship than being a perfect friend! (And it's a great social habit.) Try it next time anyone gives you feedback about something you've done.

Until you feel comfortable communicating in the moment like Cali did, give yourself full permission to take your time. Use the "Your Turn" and "Try This" exercises in this section to help you clarify your thoughts, your feelings, and what you'd like to have happen.

Talk Time

When talking seems like a good idea, ask the person involved if she can make time to meet. You can do this in person, through a call, or with a text. You could say something like "Hey, I'm hoping just the two of us can talk later today. What time works for you?"

Try to set up a time and a place that feels private and comfortable so you won't be distracted or interrupted. Even though you're upset, try to approach the other person in a respectful manner to maximize the success of your interaction.

The success of the interaction has everything to do with you expressing yourself honestly and skillfully; it doesn't depend on the other person involved. In many cases, your excellent communication will benefit both you and the relationship. In some cases, the other person involved will not have the maturity, skill, or motivation to do her part well. While that is disappointing, remind yourself that you are only in control of your part in a relationship and you are doing your best to do that part well.

Even when the three-step communication strategy is used very skillfully, some problems need more time before they can be solved. In many cases, an apology can speed up the process. An apology is often a way to get into a healing conversation and show that you want to clear the air. The gesture is also a sign that you value the relationship enough to try to save it.

The Importance of Apologizing

Remember Megan's story from the last chapter? Her entire friend group was mad at her for gossiping. Because she didn't know how to handle the situation, this is what Megan did:

Megan: At first, I tried to deny my gossiping and spread the blame on other friends who actually *did* participate in some of the gossip. I was so pissed that they took part, but I was the one taking all the blame. I didn't handle it right because everything got way worse. I ate lunch in the math room alone for over a month.

In the future, I would like to take responsibility right away and then be more directly apologetic. This drama went on way too long, and I contributed to that by trying to weasel out of just being in my tough spot and working my way out of it with more courage and honesty.

Megan learned that she needed both to take responsibility right away and to apologize. This two-step apology process is good medicine for social injury, but it took Megan awhile before she could do it.

The Two-Step Apology

1. Take responsibility for your part as soon as you're able.

2. Offer a thorough and sincere apology.

In Megan's case, she wasn't ready for the two-step apology until she did some processing with her mom. In a tearful conversation, Megan vented to her mom all the reasons why she thought the situation was unfair. Venting to a safe adult like a teacher, school counselor, or relative can be helpful because you get your feelings out and receive support from someone outside the situation who has more life experience.

Megan's mom listened as Megan talked about how difficult this friend had been—moody, rude, and flaky with texting back.

Megan felt stressed when her friend seemed nice one minute and edgy the next. "Seriously," Megan vented, "we have *all* been getting sick of her attitude. Why am I the one who is taking all the blame?"

Megan's mom listened and then offered the following suggestion: "Now that you got all that off your chest, why don't you focus on *your part* and tell me what, if anything, you could have done differently to avoid this conflict."

Feeling calmer after her "vent sesh," as she called it, Megan was ready to consider her part in the problem. She realized that she shouldn't have talked negatively to her other friends. Instead, she should have talked about her frustrations to a safe adult or written about them in her journal. She also could have talked directly to her friend about those frustrations.

After opening up to her mom, Megan felt clearer—but also anxious because now that she could see her part, she had to take responsibility and knew apologizing was the right thing to do. She was scared because she feared that if she made an apology, her friend could reject it and then Megan would feel "stupid for apologizing and also really, really rejected."

Focus on You

Megan decided to focus on what she needed to do instead of focusing on what might happen. She had hurt the feelings of several friends, and as most girls know from age four on, apologizing when you hurt someone is the right thing to do.

It is definitely scary to apologize when you're not sure that the person you're apologizing to will be open to you. It is possible that she will not be kind and understanding. It is possible that she will stay angry. But there is also a strong possibility that your apology will start a healing process. A great majority of the time that is what happens!

In the worst-case scenario, the person stays angry. At least you have the peace of mind that you did your best to bring healing to a painful situation. Your area of the garden is tidy again and that's what you can control.

Do You Want to Be Happy, or Do You Want to Be Right?

When things first blew up for Megan, she avoided apologizing for a couple of reasons. First, she was shocked and freaked out by the confrontation and the impact it had on her friend group. Second, she felt she had valid reasons for gossiping, and she believed other girls in her group agreed with her complaints about the girl she was gossiping about.

However, apologizing means you care more about the person than about the "point." In Megan's case, the "point" was her sense that she had valid reasons for gossiping and that her other friends agreed with her.

Initially, Megan cared more about her point than taking responsibility and making an apology. As she notes, she tried to "spread the blame," but that only made everything worse. In time, Megan was able to reflect on her part of the blowup, and she decided to embrace apologizing as one valuable skill in building solid relationships. Just being willing to apologize for your actions, without making excuses or blaming others, can heal friendships and make them stronger.

How to Apologize Skillfully

Before making your apology:

* Think about your part in the problem. Stay focused on *your part*, not what caused you to do what you did, and so on.

* Acknowledge (to yourself first) how your behavior may have hurt the other person. Imagine the feelings she experienced. This is called empathy.

* Make contact with the person and ask if you can speak to her alone later. Choose a good time and place for best results.

Words of Apology

If you can do it with complete honesty and no excuses for your actions, apologize personally or in a note. Face-to-face apologies are the best, because they are the most personal and complete. If you can't do that for whatever reason, you can call, write a note, or even text. The problem with texting is that it denies girls face-to-face communication. And, of course, texts can be misinterpreted.

Texting isn't the best or most personal form of communication, but if you feel unable to make a more personal apology at this point, give yourself permission to text, knowing that you are working toward in-person communication. Maybe you can follow up with an in-person interaction soon afterward.

Sample Apologies

* I've thought about what happened and I'm so sorry for my part. I feel really bad that I've hurt you.

* If I were in your shoes, I'd feel hurt too, and I want you to know I'm really sorry.

* I sincerely value our relationship, and I miss talking and hanging out with you.

* I hope you can forgive me. I can tell you with confidence that it will not happen again.

Although apologies can be very helpful in healing relationships, sometimes they can be overdone. Heed the cautionary advice below.

A Word to Overapologizers

Do you have the "Sorry, sorry, sorry" habit? You do not need to be someone who apologizes for everything. If an unexpected burp pops out during lunch, of course, you can say "Excuse me." But apologizing when you don't need to is often driven by habit, insecurity, or a need to please people all of the time. That's a lot of work!

You don't need to overapologize for social success; in fact, it may get in the way because it is often perceived as weak or needy behavior that others find annoying. Save apologies for when they are truly appropriate, authentic, and warranted.

Valuable Lessons

Megan paid a heavy price for gossiping. It was no fun for her to be left out of her social group. But in the end, she learned some valuable lessons about taking responsibility, apologizing, and making things better.

Learning to apologize also makes you more generous when it comes to receiving apologies from other people. When you know the bravery and care that goes into apologizing, you find your heart is more open when you are on the receiving end of such a gesture. Even if you're not ready to fully accept an apology from someone else, you can still thank her for the effort and let her know you will consider her words, while also giving yourself the time you need to process the situation and your feelings.

Three-step communication and two-step apologizing will also help you a lot in hard times by giving you structure to solve problems in your relationships. Practice these strategies whenever you can, and you will get better and better at communicating, especially during conflict, when it's hardest.

Keep Growing Your Communication Skills

You've learned a lot of important skills in this chapter, so keep them growing! They'll help you not only in times of conflict but in good times as well. Now let's move on to communication habits and practices that make friendships deeper and closer. Time for Tip 7: Communicate for Closeness!

Just-For-Fun Quiz: Test Your X Factor

Select the items that most describe you and write them on a piece of paper or in your tips notebook. Your answers will reveal something interesting about you. At the end of the quiz, you'll also find some suggestions for growth.

- You love a good roller coaster—the faster, the better!

- People who talk slowly drive you crazy.

- You like action-adventure flicks, horror movies, and thrillers.

- You love an exciting night out.

- You like intense sports and activities—any opportunity to go fast or push your limits.

- A lot of your meals are grab-and-go. Food is often fuel for you.

- You get scolded for interrupting and being impatient.

- Your work environment does need organizing, and you plan to get to that task as soon as time permits!

- You'll pass on the roller coaster and look for a chiller ride.

- People who talk fast wear you out.

- You like rom-coms, dramas, independent movies, and foreign films.

- You adore a warm fire and a great night's sleep.

- You like long walks or hikes in beautiful settings.

- You love good food and have an adventurous palate. You don't like to rush a meal.

- You are a great listener and are generally patient.

- You like an organized environment that pleases your sensibilities.

111

SCORING

Your X Factor is your intensity factor.

If you selected more items in the left column:

You are a thrill seeker with a passion for living life to the fullest. You like intensity and are drawn to people and experiences that make you feel fully alive and engaged.

As a thrill seeker, you never feel more alive than when things are intense and fast-moving. You are willing to be spontaneous, and aren't one to shy away from a good challenge. Sure, you may have self-doubt at times, but you deal with it by diving in and figuring things out as you go along.

Areas for growth? You may want to slow down so you can get to know interesting people who aren't necessarily as intense as you are. Mellower people are very good for you because they can introduce you to the things in life you may miss. They are also soothing because they tend to take life in stride and offer patience and perspective to hard-driving thrill seekers. If you tend to get bored easily, take a breath and be willing to go deeper—with relationships, books, assignments, and activities. Make it your mission to be a good listener. If you tend to interrupt, practice relaxing and allowing people and relationships to unfold in an unhurried manner. Sometimes you need to slow down in order to appreciate certain people and experiences that don't immediately interest you.

Also, be careful of impulsivity—meaning a tendency to jump into things without thinking through relevant details. As a thrill seeker, you may act on a whim and pay the price later. Set up structure and routine in important areas of your life, like self-care and schoolwork, and stick to it. Life will run more smoothly when you do!

If you selected more items in the right column:

You are an experience seeker with a passion for experiencing life at its richest. You're not interested in going fast. You're interested in going slowly enough to find the treasures that fast-moving thrill seekers may miss. You are very open to new ideas, people, and activities, but you're likely to observe and gather information before diving in.

Traveling to new places, eating exotic foods, and learning new things all interest you, and you have a big appetite for life and learning. You like good food, interesting locations, rich conversations, and anything you find creative and engaging. Quirky or eccentric people, activities, music, art, and fashion all please your sensibilities.

While not a slowpoke by any means, you like to savor life at a reasonable pace. When you are rushed, you become grumpy and stressed out. You'd rather move through your day efficiently but also peacefully, with a comfortable balance of quality and quantity.

As a friend, you're more likely to enjoy a walk in the rain (followed by the best cup of hot chocolate in town) than a wild night out where there could be more thrill and danger than quality moments.

Areas for growth? Keep in mind that some things in life need to get done *on* time, not *in* time. While you may prefer to arrive somewhere in your own time, other people involved may have a different requirement or expectation. Sometimes you have to sacrifice the experience you would like to have in order to be considerate to others, or to be effective in meeting responsibilities.

Also, make sure you're willing to be spontaneous and take risks—as long as they are safe and likely to be positive and beneficial. Plans are great, but sometimes going with the flow is the way to go!

tip 7

Communicate for Closeness

Like many teen girls, you may want more depth and closeness with some of your connections, yet feel unsure how to transition to that deeper place. Wanting closer connection is a sign that you desire to share your deeper self with selected others. While surface chatting is a pleasant filler in everyday life, communicating for closeness goes deeper. It involves a willingness to open up, ask questions, share thoughts and feelings, and develop a bond that feels special. Tip 7 will help you both initiate and respond to communicating for closeness so that you can experience a growing depth in a selected handful of your relationships.

To get started, let's listen to what three college girls answered in response to the question "Who are you closest to and why?"

Emme: My closest friend is my housemate who I can tell anything. She feels the same way—it's so great to have someone like that in your life.

Rosie: I have two close friends and then other friends that I hang out with but am not really close to. My close friends and I can talk about anything.

Quinn: My friend Jordan is the person I go to when things are stressful. She is totally there for me. I feel completely comfortable with her and we talk about anything and everything.

You can see in these examples that the ability to talk about *anything* is a huge value in the eyes of these girls. That makes sense, doesn't it? Being a teen girl comes with many stresses, and one of the biggest is feeling stressed about being liked and accepted. To avoid making a negative impression on others who could judge you, you might find that you hold back full expression of who you are. You might filter what you say and hold back on being the most open version of yourself. While that keeps some girls feeling "safe," it can also hinder an authentic sense of closeness. In order to feel close to others, you need to take the risk of being your true self, talking about your real thoughts and feelings, and listening with your heart to the real thoughts and feelings of the people you're getting to know.

For some girls, going to deeper levels feels comfortable, while for others, letting their guard down and communicating beyond the surface feels like a big stretch. Cate shares the challenging experiences she's had with family and friends.

✱ *Meet Cate, Age 19*

The quote that inspires her:

> *Don't walk behind me; I may not lead. Don't walk in front of me; I may not follow. Just walk beside me and be my friend.*
> —Albert Camus

I think I always wanted to communicate in a way to become close to people, but I didn't know it—and I didn't know how. I had to learn how to do it—and that happened in kind of a hard way—because in my family, we don't talk about how we feel. My family is more task oriented, or maybe you'd call it achievement oriented. My brother is like, a brain surgeon (laughs). Not really, but he actually got a perfect score on the SAT—and then there's me. I've always felt a lot of pressure and wanted to live up to his level of awesomeness.

At some point in my sophomore year, I started getting really depressed because I felt like I couldn't get the grades I wanted. I struggled to get up in the morning, I had trouble concentrating in class, I couldn't get my work done, I had a few bouts of horrible anxiety, and nothing in life seemed fun. I didn't understand what was wrong with me.

One of my friends at school asked me what was going on. I wasn't used to going deep like that and I didn't even know what to say, so I said, "Nothing." Then I missed some school, and when I came back, a couple of my friends were really loving and kind to me. They pulled me aside and told me they could tell I wasn't okay. I started crying! You need to understand, that's not me. Especially in front of people... at school!

I was embarrassed, but it also felt good. I told them how I felt everything was bad and out of control, how I felt like a loser, that all I wanted to do was sleep. And I told them that I had thoughts of not wanting to be here. Not that I'd do anything about that—but I had the thoughts.

My friends were so sweet, and they told me reassuring stuff like things would be okay and that the only thing that really mattered was that I take care of myself and get better. They walked me to our school counselor where I cried some more but also talked more.

The school counselor called my parents, who were shocked and confused, but they found me a private counselor and went to a few therapy sessions with me. I made some changes in my life to take some pressure off, but even more than that, I learned to talk about what's going on under the surface.

I have learned that talking to people you trust about your feelings is a relief, and it makes your relationship closer. My friends actually said that the whole thing helped them get to know me better because they thought I had no problems.

Having my friends there for me made me want to do the same for them, so I started working harder to be more aware of their ups and downs. I didn't hesitate to invite my friends to vent, offer hugs and encouragement, and tell them I care. Sometimes people just need to hear, "I think you're awesome and amazing and I'm here for you." It's simple when you think about it, so why hold back?

It's crazy how such a hard time for me produced such cool results. I feel like I have really valuable friends and that I am a valuable friend. I feel like my friends and I can be ridiculous and light together, but we can also be emotionally there for each other when it's needed.

My tip is this: Let yourself go beneath the surface. Ask real questions sometimes—and give real answers. It doesn't have to be a meltdown like I had. Just be willing to be more real and take risks in opening up...and helping other people to open up.

Figuring It Out

It's so true that hard times in life help us to grow. In Cate's case, the difficulty she was having created feelings of vulnerability, so when her friends approached her with love and concern, instead of playing off that she was "fine," she broke down. In that moment, Cate—a committed noncrier—was embarrassed but ultimately relieved. She recognized that it felt good to be real and even better to allow other people in so that she wasn't so alone in her experience.

Letting other people in doesn't mean that they solve your problems or take all the pain away. It means you feel less lonely in your pain! That's a really big gift to give and receive, and it creates a deeper sense of connection between people.

There are two prime lessons in Cate's story. One shows the value of letting people in and being real, even when you don't think you know how to do that. The other shows the value of being the friend who cares enough to notice, to check in, and to really be there in a kind and loving way.

Crisis and Noncrisis Communication

Fortunately, not all communication for closeness happens during a crisis such as Cate's, when she felt so bad she had thoughts of "not wanting to be here." That kind of communication revealed a *crisis situation* where there was potential harm or risk that required adult assistance. Another kind of communication, usually more common, involves a *noncrisis situation*, where there is no apparent risk of harm or danger.

To deal well with both crisis and noncrisis communication for closeness, it's important to know more about sharing personal information. It all starts with opening up, which is also called *self-disclosure.*

Self-Disclosure

Self-disclosure is sharing something personal about yourself with another person or group of people. In Cate's case, her self-disclosure was very personal and also *crisis*-level. Cate was suffering so profoundly that she had trouble functioning and had thoughts of wanting to die. Even though Cate said she wouldn't have done anything about her thoughts, the extent of her suffering made health and safety a concern.

In a crisis, get adult help. When self-disclosure suggests potential risk to health or safety, you will need to bring in additional support. Cate's friends did this by taking her to the school counselor. Here are some other examples of serious self-disclosure requiring adult help:

* self-harming behavior

* abuse behavior

* serious substance-abuse behavior

* suicidal thoughts or intent

* criminal behavior

* actions that could cause harm to the person sharing or another person

Most self-disclosure is noncrisis in nature, meaning that although the information shared may be very sad or challenging, no one is unsafe or at risk of any harm.

119

Know the Difference: Potential Risk—or Not?

It is often difficult to determine whether the self-disclosure shared is a crisis with potential harm or risk that requires adult assistance or a noncrisis situation where there is no apparent risk of harm or danger.

Teen girls who have learned the difference through real life experience describe personal situations that were either crisis or noncrisis. Read each and try to determine whether there was potential for risk or harm. Knowing the difference keeps everyone safe.

Celine: When my kitty, Holmes, got hit by a car, I was so upset. I went to my soccer game because my mom thought it would help me feel better, but the second I saw my teammates, I felt like crying again. I told a few of them and they were so nice. They were extra sweet to me and gave me hugs. It made me feel closer to them. We dedicated the game to Holmes.

Sammi: My aunt got sick with cancer and my mom was upset and gone a lot my freshman year of high school. It was a double stress for me 'cause I love my aunt and also I'm used to having my mom there for me. I opened up to some of my friends. In general, I like to keep to myself about sad stuff and I don't like to be a burden, but I've learned that it feels good to get support and to give it, too.

Aimee: My mom and my sister have what you would call a volatile relationship—lots of yelling. I let a couple of my friends know that home was stressful and that I need a break sometimes from being there. Those friendships became closer because of that. And those friends opened up more to me, too.

Sophia: I could tell one of my friends was getting weird with food and dieting. She became obsessed with calories and weight. I asked her about it and really kind of pushed her one day because I was getting worried. She confessed that she was purging daily, and I felt overwhelmed and scared for her. Even though she didn't want me to tell anyone, I told my mom and my mom talked to her mom. In the short term, it was stressful, but in the bigger picture, it was good 'cause now she is getting help and we are closer friends.

Morgan: I have a friend who shared a lot, and I've got to say that she stressed me out. I care about her, but I feel unqualified to handle some of what's going on with her—like sneaking out at night, meeting up with people she hardly knows, partying out of control. We have a teacher who is really cool, so I talked to her about feeling worried and overwhelmed about my friend. She confirmed for me that it was a serious situation and that it was too big for me to handle that info on my own. She let me know that she would very gently talk to that friend and get some support on board. I was grateful because it took me out of that role, and my friend got the real support she needed.

Arianna: I struggled with depression and anxiety for a while. I felt like if things didn't get better, I would kill myself. I texted my friend one night and told her how I was feeling. She told her mom and her mom called my mom. At the time, I really didn't want any of that to happen, but I can see it was all for my own good. Now I'm in therapy and getting the help I need. I have hope now, and I feel things are getting better.

Crisis Sharing

In the last case, Arianna self-disclosed personal information that was clearly crisis level because her safety was at risk. Her friend made a responsible decision to get adults involved, and the situation improved for Arianna as a result.

Sophia and Morgan were recipients of crisis-level information that overwhelmed them, and understandably so. In situations where someone's safety and wellness are in question, you need to get a trusted adult involved. Parents, teachers, school counselors, doctors, and coaches are usually good people to go to. For the good of the person in crisis and for your own good, make sure to involve trusted, caring adults as soon as possible.

Some girls resist getting others involved and keep the weight of a friend in distress on their shoulders alone. Even if you're the "therapist" in your group of friends, this is too big a responsibility for you! Your friend is not the only one experiencing the stress of her situation—you are, too, and you also matter. Plus, even though you have great intentions to be helpful, you're not trained in crisis-level intervention. Take care of both yourself and your friend. Get an adult to help. As Sophia notes, in the short term, a friend might be mad that you consulted an adult; but in the big picture, that important decision gets your friend the qualified help she needs.

Noncrisis Sharing

Celine, Sammi, and Aimee talked about self-disclosing to friends about very difficult events and situations. In each case, their willingness to open up and be real created both support and greater closeness. Sammi and Aimee even noted that their self-disclosures paved the way for their friends to open up too so everyone became more open. Though Celine, Sammi, and Aimee were struggling with hard situations, no one was unsafe or in danger, and additional support was not required.

Tips for Self-Disclosure

To start exploring communicating for closeness, here are some tips from young women in college who have had some useful social experience in this area:

Shay: When you don't know someone very well, start with small self-disclosures and not the biggest, gnarliest thing you could share. That way you don't feel overexposed and you don't make the other person uncomfortable either.

Marley: Sometimes when you are on the verge of becoming good friends with someone, you might want to have more elevated conversations about more intense topics but are scared to initiate them. My advice is that if you feel like you're getting close with someone, don't be afraid to start those conversations like "What do you think happens after we pass away?" or whatever. She will most likely be interested in talking to someone new like you about your views

123

on big topics, especially in the teenage years when kids are starting to figure out how they feel about politics, religion, life! It can be a positive experience to talk to someone else and have a cool discussion. Then you feel closer knowing you had a conversation about something meaningful and not just the typical small talk.

Kendall: I'm from the UK and we all took a Communication class in school where I learned about self-disclosure. Basically, it taught about being reciprocal so when someone shares something personal, not right in that moment but at some point, you do the same and then you build mutual closeness that strengthens your relationship. I've always kept that in mind. Sometimes when I know someone for a while and think they're friend material, I initiate self-disclosure by telling them something more personal, like how I miss England and how things are different here. Being a bit vulnerable tends to make other people feel comfortable and open up to you more.

Jade: When you receive a self-disclosure that's very personal or intense, avoid what I call the "scramble." The scramble means you're so worried about saying the right thing that you aren't really there in the right way with your heart and your attitude. It doesn't matter what you *say* really, so don't get distracted by trippin' on yourself. Get more into *feeling* compassion for the person and let things be natural. When someone is really hurting or gets really personal, she just wants to see that you are listening and that you care. I literally tell myself in my mind, *Jade, you don't have to* do *anything except* be *here—open and caring.* The person isn't even waiting for you to say the perfect thing, so don't scramble—just be there.

Scout: I think most people feel offended when they're sharing and the listener wants to give a solution. In your mind, you're thinking either *I know that already, do you think I'm stupid?* or *You really don't get it.* The absolute *worst* thing is when the listener changes the focus to something about her and takes over. I hate that! I know one girl who does that and I wouldn't open up to her if she were the last person on Earth. It's annoying and hurtful.

Paige: Using pet names adds a flavor of closeness. My friends and I called each other nicknames and pet names. You just need to make sure you really feel it and that the other person isn't annoyed by it. My friend Catherine loves being called Kitty Cat on occasion, but my friend Isabelle wants to be called Isabelle and nothing else.

Dahlia: When you're in high school, you so want to fit in and be cool, but then you learn that being a dork, not taking yourself too seriously, making a joke about yourself, or being silly puts other people at ease and promotes closeness and realness.

McKenna: My favorite tip for creating closeness is a habit I got into in college. Girls are way more positive than in high school, and now I'll go up to someone and say, "Bella, we were just talking about how awesome you are." So, in other words, you *tell* people nice things that they wouldn't otherwise know—nice things you've heard or said, or that that person's name came up and there was all this positive energy toward them. I *love* it when people share that stuff with me because I automatically feel accepted and appreciated, and it makes the connection easier and closer.

Your Turn: Practicing Self Disclosure

Now it's your turn to look at how you might include or increase self-disclosure in your relationships. Pull out a piece of paper or your tips notebook to record your thoughts and answers.

1. Review what the girls above shared and write down a few tips that you'd like to try. List as many tips as you want.

2. Think of people you'd like to try your tips on. Write down as many names as you'd like.

3. Set a goal to try out a tip (or two or three) in the next week. Try at least one tip and more if you're motivated.

Yay You!

In this chapter, you have explored how to communicate in ways that enhance closeness and intimacy in teen girl relationships. Some of these were how to be be open and honest with others, how to practice appropriate self disclosure, and how to determine the difference between crisis and noncrisis communication. Your next tip focuses on your online social life. Tip 8: Be

Your Best Self in Social Media and Texting supports you in being the person you want to be, right where a lot of socializing happens—online!

Just-For-Fun Quiz: Find Your Place in Nature

Are you a rock, a river, or a sunset? Find out which category of nature best describes your friendship style.

Rate the following statements on a scale of 1 to 5. A 1 indicates that the statement does not describe you at all, a 3 indicates that it moderately describes you, and a 5 indicates that it strongly describes you. Write your answers on a piece of paper or in your tips notebook.

Rock

- You are solid and steadfast. When you make a friend, you tend to stick with that person.

- You always try to do the right thing. When you don't, you can be unforgiving with yourself.

- If you make a plan, you tend to keep it. Flaking frustrates you.

- You may get annoyed with others, but you don't bail when times get tough.

- The people you care about know you care. You don't necessarily gush love—you show it through the overall stability of your friendship.

- You don't tend to be dramatic. In fact, others look to you to be a sensible and stabilizing force in dramatic situations.

- You say what you mean and mean what you say. You are incapable of being fake, and you steer clear of others who strike you as inauthentic.

- You sometimes feel more adult than you actually are. Other people comment that you are mature or "an old soul."

River

- You like variety in people, places, music, food, and style.

- You get bored with same old, same old. You like change.

- You would rather feel interested and entertained than safe and comfortable.

- You would rather do something out in public or in nature than have a long, deep conversation in a coffee shop.

- Sometimes people feel like you have blown them off for something better, but you wish people would be more flexible and in-the-moment, like you are.

- You'd rather show that you care by spending time with someone and having fun than telling the person how you feel or opening up and getting personal.

- You don't mind changing friends when things don't work out. You like meeting new people and feeling interested.

- Sometimes you can't understand why other people are freaking out because you have a high tolerance for new situations and change in general.

Sunset

- Sometime people your age strike you as shallow and ridiculous. You crave people who "get it."

- Even as a child, you thought a lot about big concepts, like life, death, the world, and eternity.

- You would much rather talk about an idea or a philosophical concept than gossip.

- You'd rather have a few deep friendships than many superficial acquaintances.

- You do not kill spiders. They have families and lives, too!

- You look for people you can count on and who really "get" you.

- You look for meaning in life, and you connect best with people who are philosophical, spiritual, or intellectual.

- You want to have a job that makes the world a better place.

- You are attracted to friends who are smart, wise, and growth-oriented.

Keep in mind that you might identify with more than one category, or even all three! Here are qualities associated with each:

If you identify most with the rock:

You are the ultimate antidrama queen. When someone needs you, you take pride in being there in a steady and caring way. If a drama queen sweeps into your life, you disappear because you have no patience for self-created chaos. You like being social, but on a deep level—nothing wild or out of control for you. You tend to get respect from other people who see you as stable and "together," trustworthy and authentic. *Take Note:* You may need to add some silliness and play to your life. There may be reasons you are so steadfast, and you may take on too much adult responsibility. You don't have to change anything drastically—just make sure you allow yourself to be a kid still, because you are!

If you identify most with the river:

You have an appetite for life and adventure. You like going places and trying new things. You bond with people by sharing life with them. While you don't mind talking, you're not one to sit in a coffee shop talking for hours. You'd rather be at a concert dancing and enjoying the music with people who are fun to be with. While you care about people, you accept that things change, and you know that the people you get along with at one point in your life may not suit you as well at another time. *Take Note:* Others may get more attached to you than you are to them. Remember to be conscientious of their feelings. Your flair for loving life and being in the moment attracts other people to you—you model a love for life for them!

If you identify most with the sunset:

Just as a beautiful sunset illuminates the sky, for you, so can friendship. While you like fun, depth in a friendship is what feeds you. You are therefore attracted to people who are rich and deep and who can talk about things you consider important. People who don't "get" the bigger picture of life sometimes feel shallow or immature to you, and leave you feeling lonely or frustrated. You enjoy getting to know people who seem aware and engaged environmentally, politically, or spiritually. You seek to make a difference in the world and to consort with others who are on the same path. *Take Note:* You may not find a lot of people like you right now. Seek out classes, books, clubs, and activities that help you connect to your interests and meet people who share them!

tip 8

Be Your Best Self on Social Media and While Texting

No matter how old you were when tech devices entered your life, you're probably a fan. Why wouldn't it be love at first sight for a little girl—what's more fun than playing with mom's cell phone when you're bored? Remember those days of ancient phone technology? That first phone you played with probably couldn't even take photos!

Magically, those phones kept changing and evolving while your roles reversed and you became the teacher to the adults in your life—doing your very best to be patient with their difficulty catching on. As soon as you could make it happen, you got one yourself. Chances are that right this moment, your phone is closer to you than your toes!

In the tech universe, kids learn faster than adults and often navigate without supervision. (Why ask for permission when they don't even know that what you're doing online exists?) Unlike cruising around the playground where adults intervene when socializing turns rough, the tech universe can go from nice to nasty in a single tap—and no one's there to guide you.

As one teen girl shares, "I've been caught up in online drama that ruined my social life," and another admits, "I'm guilty of saying things through text that I would never say if I were to have a face-to-face talk with someone. It's like, I get fake brave in the worst way possible."

Tip 8 comes your way from some teens just out of high school who wish they could serve on an official committee to help younger teens avoid making the same mistakes they did. Several of these teens noted that much of what they learned about tech tips, they learned the hard way.

As eighteen-year-old Georgie shares:

My parents told me things like "Don't text during dinner" and "Don't sleep with your phone under your pillow." Like most teenagers, I tried to get away with both of those things, but I had no one to warn me: "Hey Georgie, anything you text may be forwarded to ten or a million other people" or "The photos you're posting are giving the world the wrong impression of you."

I made both of those mistakes myself, and as much as I learned from them, I'd be very happy to help other girls avoid them. Of course, even if my parents had told me those things, I wouldn't have listened because this is an area you really need young adult consultants. Because we just recently went through it all, we can help young girls avoid easy-to-make mistakes.

How to Be Your Best Tech Self

Jadon, 19, kicks off Tip 8 by noting what it's like to grow up with social media and how teens communicate with technology differently (and more wisely) as they get older.

When you're a young teenager, it's common to use social networking to build popularity. You get as many friends and followers as possible, and getting "likes" for what you post means everything to you. It can get obsessive. I guess you could say it's all quantity and not much quality. The quantity of friends, followers, likes, shares, reblogs, and so forth makes you feel good about yourself for like, a minute. It's not real self-esteem, so it doesn't last long.

I feel like teens are very vulnerable to getting obsessed with and addicted to social media. I went through that stage and there's nothing good about it. What you really want as a young teen is to feel good about yourself because being accepted is the most important thing you can think of. It's just too easy to try to impress other people for the instant gratification of getting "likes" and then checking out who liked your post. You see people you know, people you hardly know, and people you may have crushes on "like" what you post and you're on top of the world.

Or you don't see people "like" your post and you feel crushed and your day is ruined. I remember being thirteen, fourteen, and fifteen, and my emotions were already a mess most of the time. Social media did not help with that. High, low, high, low—it's just not good.

As you get older, you start to want only actual friends on your sites. You don't care as much about likes and so on, because you realize how meaningless that kind of "popularity" is. You trade in quantity for quality, because it feels more real and fulfilling.

Having the people you care about care about you builds real self-esteem, I think. And it feels great to be someone's real friend, as opposed to feeling great because your new profile pic got lots of likes. Life is better when the world isn't your potential fan club anymore. That said, I have a few recommendations that I wish I'd known a few years ago.

Don't think of social networking as the place to build your popularity.

If you do, you'll get caught up in styling an image of yourself and your life that makes you look "good" to other people. It's just too manipulative and fake, and it will get you thinking about everything in life in terms of how it will appear on social networking—what kind of reaction it will get. Popularity is never a good focus in your social life. Focus on being yourself and work on real relationships—quality not quantity—in your real life.

Do think of social networking as a way to stay in touch with your friends.

It's especially good for people you don't see every day. I try to keep track of what's going on with my long-distance friends and family by seeing what they post and commenting so they feel me there even though I'm not physically there. I post things that show them about my life, so if I go to a music festival or something, they'll be in the loop. I do not post to look cool or create an image. At this point, I'd rather really be who I am than create some image of who I want people to think I am.

Do express your true self on social media.

It's easy to want to impress people, but avoid that and figure out ways to post or share something that communicates who your authentic self is. If you love taking photos of your cat, share that. If you are the best cupcake baker you know, share the recipe. Stay you! The feedback you get for being you feels so much better than the feedback you get for making yourself into someone who gets "likes" and new followers.

Do ask yourself the question, "What can I offer as a friend to other people today?"

That guideline will get you thinking of something you can share that inspires people or makes them laugh. Or think about whose post you can make a positive comment on—wishing someone a warm happy birthday with a personalized note about why she is special to you, things like that. It will save you from thinking of yourself as a product to promote online and instead get you thinking about what kind of friend you can be.

Do push yourself to make a sincere comment when you decide to comment and go beyond the basic and superficial.

It's good practice, it's great for relationships, and people feel the difference. This is especially important to do when the person is a good friend or someone you would like to be a good friend. It builds a feeling of closeness that you can build on in real life.

Pull Back on Posting

The idea that younger teens need guidance about what they post receives strong agreement from Adelle, 19. Here is what she has to say:

I wish I could be a big sister to some of the younger teens using social media. I have two younger sisters and since I live at home, I see their social media posts regularly. I make sure I see them.

I am so disturbed by the pictures girls post. Young teens want validation and attention so much that I think they are prone to posting shots of themselves that send the wrong message.

Sure, they may get a lot of "likes" when they post overly sexy pics of themselves in bathing suits or revealing tops, but it's not the right kind of attention. Trust me, being considered "hot" by other people is not a good goal for you. You're better than that, and you have more to offer than a sexy appearance.

That's what I tell my sisters who are sucked into this culture. I also tell them, "You won't ever regret not posting a skanky pic—but you will regret posting it." In other words, you don't regret not posting, so you're better off being cautious than brave when it comes to social media.

This is what I recommend to my sisters and all girls:

Don't post any photo of yourself you wouldn't frame and give to your grandma.

I'm not kidding—use that as a guideline and you'll be fine. Human beings were here for a long time before they decided it would be a great idea to take pictures of themselves all of the time, wherever they go—and share those pictures with the world.

136

Do put yourself on selfie restriction if you post more than two per week.

Since I'm a lot older than my sisters, and they look up to me, I help them use good judgment by advising them to post only one selfie a week, and they can only post it if it passes the "grandma test." I think this saves them from being obsessed with taking selfies, and in a bigger sense, just obsessed with themselves. Instead of posting photos of yourself, post pictures that are funny or interesting. Push yourself creatively to take nature shots or artsy shots. When you put your own image out there too much, you look shallow and possibly desperate for attention.

Do open your mind to being more mysterious— less overexposed.

It makes people curious about you! It protects you from being labeled. Social media can be a really rough world, so protect yourself from being one of its victims.

Before moving on to more insights from the "committee," let's pause to talk about a common teen affliction that may affect the way you use technology: FOMO.

FOMO: Fear of Missing Out

As you energize new guidelines for your technology, you may notice it's a struggle, especially if you are currently spending a lot of time on social media. FOMO, or fear of missing out, may poke, prod, and torture you, driving you back to bad habits you are trying to modify. You can get through the pain of FOMO considering this perk: When you impose guidelines for yourself, the adults in your life are less likely to do it for you. (They won't need to.)

Sometimes parents restrict or eliminate social media time for teens because they are worried that teens are distracted from schoolwork and other responsibilities. When restriction occurs, you may suffer in ways that surprise you. Maybe you can you relate to what this fourteen-year-old teen shares:

Tessa: I've never done drugs, but I can imagine what withdrawal feels like because when I'm grounded from social media, I swear I crave it. I feel urges to check my sites and see what's going on. I feel like not being online is going to hurt me socially, even though I know that's not true. I get irritable, I'm not nice to be around, and my mood is terrible. I feel like I'm missing out.

While Tessa's suffering is real, over time, an interesting thing often happens. She joins other teen girls who find that a break in social media releases them from obsessive preoccupation. Tessa continues:

> I don't like to admit this to my parents—and trust me, I don't—but getting a break from social media feels great after the first two days. I start feeling happier, less stressed, less obsessive. I remember that I like to do other things, like drawing and playing the piano—even simple stuff like playing with my puppy. I get a better perspective about what's real and what's important. It's like, when you're immersed in that world, it feels so real and addictive, but when you're out of it, it honestly looks kind of lame.

Try This: Take a Vacay

How do you feel about giving yourself a break from social media? Are you willing to try it as an experiment to see how a break affects your mood and the way you spend your time? Many other teens have found that taking a social media break actually helps their social life because they reallocate that focus to real-life relationships. Here are three ideas:

1. **Take a week off.** Yes, an entire week—seven days. Think of it as an experiment and keep notes on what you observe about yourself. It may be hard at first, but you can do it! Like lots of other girls, you may find yourself putting more energy into other things, including homework, creative projects, and in-person relationships.

    After your week off, take a good, honest look at what improved in your life when social media didn't distract you. You may want to take one week off per month!

2. **Give yourself a social media time limit.** Ideally, you'll try this after your one-week social media break. These two suggestions go great together because after a one-week break, your time limit won't feel so restrictive.

    The best way to use a time limit is to set your phone alarm or a stop watch for fifteen minutes. Then give yourself that amount of time to be online and be strict with yourself. Instead of getting lost and having an hour pass as if it were five minutes, you will be more disciplined and thoughtful about how and where you spend your social networking time.

    As one teen notes, "If I set an alarm on my phone for fifteen minutes on social media, I use social media differently. I don't lurk on other people's pages, I don't post much myself, and I just keep it light and fast. It keeps me on track so I know what's going on, but I don't waste time or get sucked in."

3. **Learn to snap shut**. Anytime you're on social media and you start to feel insecure, anxious, depressed, jealous, or worried, *snap shut* your laptop or whatever device you have turned on and get away from what you're doing. You can actually become extremely good at this (even the most addicted girls agree), and you will feel so much more control over your mood.

There is no reason to stay on whatever site you're on when it negatively affects your mood. After you snap shut, try doing something completely different and upbeat, like calling a friend or engaging in a pleasant activity.

And Then Try This: Personalize Guidelines

Create any additional guidelines that will help you where you need help. For some girls, it's giving themselves a limit on how often they post. If you post less, your overall social media involvement will be light. Light users have more time to do other things, such as nurture real-life relationships and succeed at avoiding the social drama that comes with heavier use.

For other girls, a good guideline is to post two or fewer selfies a week. While pictures of yourself can be fun to take, posting selfies too often can make you come across as self-absorbed. As many teen girls will readily tell you, no one wants a newsfeed full of some girl's photo shoot. Girls who post selfies too often are targets for criticism.

Guidelines should be personalized because every girl knows how and where she gets "sucked in." For one teen, checking who else "liked" the photos of guys she had crushes on became an obsession. She checked the "likes" and followed up by investigating names that came up (sometimes referred to as "lurking"). Her experience:

> *My insecurity reached insane levels with this habit, so I had to be very disciplined to stop myself. I'm obsessive anyway, so less social media is definitely better for me. Not checking who else is liking posts is my personal guideline, and I have to stick to it strictly.*

Your Turn: Create Your Own Guidelines

What additional guidelines would you like to create for yourself? On a piece of paper or in your tips notebook, write them down and stick to them. Notice what improves for you when you stick to your guidelines.

More on Being Your Best Tech Self

The "committee" members agree that a lot of bad social manners take place on cell phones. They feel it makes sense, because it's common for teen girls to struggle with moodiness. When you're moody, easily annoyed, and communicating without having to look someone in the eye, problems are bound to arise.

And who annoys teen girls more than anybody else? Other than teachers, parents, and siblings—each other!

It's very common for teen girls to care about each other and, at the same time, become easily irritated with one another, especially younger teens. Hence, the friend you love one moment might infuriate you the next, prompting a rude text you later wish you could take back.

Put Your Thumbs on Restriction

A huge problem, according to Kaila, is that cell phones offer a much too easy way to communicate the irritations that come and go all day. Because you can text, and escape the reality check of seeing how your communication impacts the receiver, it's easy to be harsher than you should be.

For this reason, Kaila has come up "the twenty-four-hour rule" to help avoid unnecessary conflict through texting.

My perspective about text communication is that lacking face-to-face contact makes girls ruder than they otherwise would be. When you're face-to-face and annoyed, you filter yourself because you feel really personally responsible for what you say. You don't have that connection when texting, so you say something rude or sarcastic and "tap," it's sent.

It's like a hit-and-run because you don't witness the damage you just caused. I think girls get annoyed with each other a lot and don't necessarily want to have a confrontation face-to-face. But what feels good for a second becomes complicated and just not worth it.

This is what I recommend:

Don't send anything when you're annoyed.

On a piece of paper, write exactly what you feel like texting. That way, the urge to express yourself is satisfied, but no one is hurt. The next day, read it and see if you still feel compelled to communicate whatever you wrote. Most of the time, you won't. You'll be over it and relieved that you didn't stir up bad feelings for nothing. Bunch up the paper and throw it away. It's great symbolism, and you're teaching yourself self-discipline, which will definitely help your relationships.

Do wait twenty-four hours and if, in that time, you still feel annoyed, call that person and say you want to talk to her about something.

Communicate as well as you can by showing respect for the other person and yourself. That way things will get worked out instead of becoming even worse. (See Tip 6: Communicate Through Conflict for a reminder about communication in times of conflict.)

Drawing from her personal experiences with friends, Gwen, 18, adds to rules about rude texting:

What I've found is that people argue more respectfully and intelligently when they're in each other's physical company. Even talking on the phone is better than texting. When texting, there is just not enough awareness and accountability for the emotions getting stirred up—plus you can't read the emotions the person is feeling without hearing her voice or seeing her face. My advice:

Don't argue through text—at all.

I have seen people have long, drawn out arguments all through text, and it all gets more tangled and complicated than it needs to be because of the inability to read emotions through text.

***Do* use texting to tell someone you'd like to talk if you want.**

If someone is trying to have an argument over text, say something like "I think this conversation would be more productive in person" or even on the phone.

Never–Instead Rules

The "committee" leaves you with this list of "never–insteads," which is a concept they made up. Read on for these closing guidelines:

NEVER	INSTEAD
Text and drive.	Put your phone on silent, so you won't be tempted to answer.
Spend time with friends, but give more time to your phone than to them.	*Be* with who you are *with*, and put your phone aside. It's rude and hurtful, whether your friend calls you out on it or not. Don't use "she's on her phone, too" an an excuse; she might be on her phone because you are and she just doesn't want to confront you.

Forget that any snapshots taken can be forwarded to the world and kept forever.

Assume that everything you say or send can be distributed to the world, including your grandma. It's happened a lot. You don't need to be that girl with huge regrets.

Say too much personal stuff through text because it makes the real relationship feel awkward.

Force yourself to create a relationship in real life that progresses one step at a time. If it all happens through text (or online), things feel out of pace in person, and it might make a real relationship harder, not easier.

Your Turn: Adding More Tips

Are there any tips you would add? Think about what you and your friends would say if you formed a committee to help younger girls. Write your tips on a piece of paper or in your tips notebook.

Are you online friends with (or following) a younger teen girl who may be bringing trouble to herself because of what she's posting? Maybe there's a way you could gently give her the feedback she needs to use better judgment. She's more likely to listen and respect a teen who is caring and who has "been there."

Think It Over

Now you know how to keep yourself in a good zone with social media. Integrating the tips you just learned will help you maintain high quality and low drama in your social life. You will find that you're protected from some of the chaos you see other people experience. Now you're ready to learn what teens have to say about another topic, overthinking, in Tip 9: Be More and Think Less.

Just-For-Fun Quiz: Check Your Social Media Status

How often do you use social media? Select the answer that best fits you and write the corresponding number down on a piece of paper or in your tips notebook.

1. You check it every once in a while. It's useful for staying in touch with distant friends, and it can be fun sometimes.

2. You check it every day, without fail. Thanks to your statuses, Snapchats and tweets, your friends are usually aware of what you're doing, who you're with, and what your latest meal looked like.

3. You are permanently glued to your phone—in the car, at meals, under your desk in class. You *have* to be ready if a new notification comes through. Your phone buzzes nonstop with messages, which makes you feel popular and wanted.

You post a new picture that you thought looked really good, but it only gets one "like." How does this make you feel?

1. Whatever, it's no big deal. You hope that your friends got a chance to see the picture because you looked really cute, but one photo out of the trillions on the Internet doesn't matter.

2. Well, that's disappointing. You can't believe that no one is giving your beautiful picture the attention it deserves. Not even that creepy guy who always likes your photos liked it. What if it doesn't look as good as you thought?

3. When you check your phone and see that there's no new notifications, your heart sinks. You start to have a major self-esteem crash. If nobody liked your photo, doesn't that mean nobody likes you?

Imagine that you're having a rough day. How does it make you feel to see a photo album of a group of your Facebook friends having fun on the beach?

1. You wish you could have been there, of course, but you're happy that your friends got to have some fun. You make a mental note to hang out with them soon.

2. You feel a little twinge of jealousy—maybe that you weren't invited, or that they were having fun without you. But the feeling soon passes.

3. You start to turn on yourself, feeling down about your own life. Why don't you get out more and go to the beach? They all look so happy in the pictures, while you're sitting at home miserable.

You tell yourself you'll start your homework at 5 p.m. You're browsing Facebook to relax, when you look up at the clock and see that it's already 6:15. Do you:

1. Freak out, shut down your browser immediately, and get started in a rush?

2. Tell yourself that you already went past your deadline, so you might as well wait until 7. That's a nice round number—best to just wait until then and start fresh.

3. Double down, open up Twitter and Tumblr, and keep browsing to distract yourself from the anxiety of the deadline.

You've been on vacation with no phone service, and haven't been able to get online all week. How do you feel without Facebook and social media access?

1. In the back of your mind, you wonder what you've missed on your Facebook wall, but you don't really think too much about it. Maybe you remind yourself to post some pictures when you get back.

2. You're constantly checking your phone by instinct, forgetting that you don't have service. You feel frequent urges to refresh Facebook, are constantly thinking of things you can post to get more "likes," and generally feel like a big part of your life is missing.

3. You insist that your parents take you to an Internet café so you can get online. When they refuse, you start to get really upset.

SCORING

Add up all of the numbers you wrote down and find out what your score says about your social media use.

5–7 points:

Social media is a tool that you use to make your life better—staying in touch with friends, keeping up to date on what's happening in your social circle, and having a laugh every once in a while. Your use of it is pretty healthy and normal.

8–12 points:

You might go a little overboard on social media sometimes. But hey, we all spend a ton of time online these days. It's not the worst thing in the world, right? Right. But still, when used in excess, social media can be addictive and can have a big impact on your well-being. Think about it: everyone posts their best selves on social media—their best photos, their coolest experiences. You're seeing everyone else's highlight reel, not their real lives, and it's easy to feel like your own life doesn't stack up.

13–15 points:

Heavy social media use has made you really attached to it. Sometimes you feel like your self-worth is tied to how many followers you get. When you're away from your phone, you think about it constantly. Getting "likes" on social media can make or break your day. Try to take a step back from these websites, and remember that no matter how many "friends" you have on Facebook, you're so much more than that number. Social media is just a game. You live in the real world, not on a website, and you're a valuable person with a ton to offer.

tip 9

Be More and Think Less

Since you were little, you've been encouraged to *think* well, to *think* clearly, to *think* before you act, to *think* about the consequences of your actions, to *think* about how other people feel, to *think* about what other people want, to make sure people *think* positively about you, and to make good choices—which also requires *thinking*.

What you probably did not learn about thinking is that it can go overboard. There is definitely such a thing as too much thinking, and if you're like a lot of girls your age, you've experienced it.

Too much thinking, also known as *overthinking, obsessing,* or *ruminating,* is a common affliction that causes a lot of suffering for people of all ages. For teen girls, overthinking often arises in the context of their social lives.

Can you relate to any of these girls?

* I have trouble sleeping at night because I keep thinking and thinking about every social interaction that happened that day.

* My mind feels like it's driven by a motor that I can't turn off. I obsess about how I come across to other

people and what they think about me, and the more I obsess, the worse I feel.

* I think so much about what I might have said that sounded stupid that I make myself feel sick.

* I often wonder and worry that I hurt someone's feelings, sounded rude or stupid, or embarrassed myself.

* When I'm in a group of people, I feel paralyzed by the possibility of making a mistake, so I'm a freakin' mute—or I try to join the conversation but feel extremely awkward.

* If I could just turn my thoughts off for a second, I could feel normal around other people and have more fun.

Notice how overthinking is usually negative. Have you ever obsessed about all the wonderful things that have happened or may happen in your social life? How amazing you are and how everyone likes you? Probably not. The content of overthinking is usually driven by insecurity, self-doubt, and fear, which makes it negative.

The rise of these feelings in your teen years is completely normal and makes sense from a developmental standpoint. At your age, being liked and accepted is a major priority. It's natural and developmentally appropriate to be less interested in bonding with your parents and more interested in bonding with your friends. With this transition in focus comes some level of insecurity because the social stakes seem higher—being accepted and liked feels more important.

By the time most girls get to middle school, they start to become aware of social acceptance—who has it and who doesn't. To have it feels like a confirmation that you're okay by a bunch of new standards that weren't important in elementary school. There are so many changes in the way you look, think, and feel that social acceptance makes it seem like you're okay and life is okay. Any other possibility is understandably terrifying and girls want to avoid it at all costs.

Fear stimulates the mind into thinking (thinking, thinking) as a way to figure out where you stand socially and how you're doing as a likeable and acceptable person.

When your mind floods you with thinking, worrying, replaying interactions, and more thinking, it may feel like you are trying to "get" somewhere with all that mental activity so that you can experience relief. It's as if you believe that thinking will help you feel better, that overthinking is going to be productive.

It isn't. Overthinking keeps you from being present and connected to other people. It separates you from your best self and from other people by distracting you with worry and uncomfortable self-absorption. For example, it's hard to be a good listener capable of interaction when you're consumed with the fear of not being annoying.

In this chapter, you will learn how to identify overthinking, acknowledge what has triggered it, and redirect your focus in more positive ways. As you use the strategies in this chapter, you will notice that you get better at trusting who you are and what you're doing moment to moment, no matter what social situation you're in. You will succeed in thinking less and *being* more.

This is a perfect time to meet Gemma, who worked hard to pull back on overthinking. Here's what Gemma has to say.

✱ *Meet Gemma, Age 18*

The quotes that inspire her:

> *Thinking is good. Overthinking can end things before they ever get the chance to develop.* —Dorothy Rosenberg

> *Get out of your head and get into your heart.*
> *Think less, feel more.* —Osho

Gemma is a high school senior who learned tricks to tame her overthinking. Having more power over her thinking habits helped Gemma feel better about herself and her social life.

I was a little shy as a kid, but I wasn't out of control with overthinking then. When you are very young, I think you just assume other people are okay with you, unless they let you know directly that they're not.

Then you get into middle school and several things change. You care way more about being accepted. You want people to think you're pretty and smart and sporty. And most of all, you want people to like you and accept you.

At the same time, in middle school, if people have a problem with you, they don't necessarily tell you. They just shut you out. This was really bad for me because it made me start to worry—okay, obsess—about what people really thought of me. Sure, they would act nice to me, or neutral, but did they really like me?

If ever someone wasn't nice, maybe not mean but just preoccupied or indifferent toward me, I would take it personally and worry. I made things that probably weren't about me all about me.

I remember one girl who seemed really pretty and nice and kind of socially powerful to me. I so wanted to be her friend—it was kind of pathetic. No matter how hard I tried, she and her friends just kinda kept me out of their group. They weren't horrible, they just didn't let me be a part of their thing.

Every day, I'd come home and obsess about it. I'd try to talk to my mom, but I think I burned her out on the topic because she'd get impatient with how anxious and miserable I was. She talked to my aunt about my overthinking, and my aunt suggested I learn meditation because meditation helps you slow down your thoughts.

We couldn't find a meditation class, so my mom bought me a CD and I started listening to it. Meditation was hard at first, and, honestly, I fell asleep to the CD most of the time. I'm still not an awesome meditator, but I've learned some concepts about my mind and thinking that have helped me a lot, such as your thoughts aren't necessarily true and you can release them.

I also learned that we have tons and tons of thoughts, and most of them are not helpful to our lives or well-being. Most of them aren't even important in any way—they're just clutter. The problem happens when we get all carried away with our thoughts and think that they're accurate when, a lot of the time, they come from fear and insecurity.

With all of this information, I began to identify my problem thoughts and give them less attention. Another thing that happened is that I gave up trying to be accepted by groups of girls that were not interested in me.

To this day, I don't overwork to make girls who aren't that nice or open to me like me. Not everyone likes everyone— that's life, and it's fine with me now. I've been really happy socially hanging with a group of girls that are really good people—we all care about each other and are there for each other.

Meditation has been helpful to me and I recommend it, but I think you can improve your overthinking even without meditation.

Figuring It Out

When overthinking strikes, you may feel trapped in obsessive loops of worry that don't go anywhere and don't bring anything—except anxiety. In order to take back your power, it helps to understand your mind and how it works.

As weird as this suggestion sounds, think of your mind as a puppy. Like most puppies, it can be a hot mess of lively troublemaking—until you give it a bit of training.

Train Your Puppy

In the training process, there is you (the trainer) and your mind (the puppy). Start by appreciating that, as the trainer, you are a complex person with many different parts that all come together to make you *you*. Your mind is one of your parts—the part of your brain that thinks—and, for the purposes of this chapter, it's your puppy.

To keep a puppy safe as it explores the world, you may want to use a retractable leash, the kind that can be very long or, with the push of a button, become short to bring the puppy closer. *Skunk ahead?* No problem. Push the button and keep your puppy from an unfortunate encounter. You can push that button at any time while you gently train your puppy to stay away from explorations that will only cause trouble.

As with your frisky puppy's leash, you have the power to push the *retract* button on your *mind* and reel in overthinking. The first step is to notice when you are overthinking. Many teens figure it out because they know how to identify the feelings of insecurity and worry, which tangle in with overthinking.

Insecurity and worry often trigger overthinking and keep it going, making you feel worse and worse the longer overthinking continues. While feeling bad is not fun, you can begin to recognize those terrible feelings and connect them with this question: "Wait, am I overthinking right now?"

Next, to retract that leash, pay attention to what is actually going on in the moment, in observable, physical reality. Thoughts are happening in your head, and because you're overthinking, they are sending little stress grenades down to your body where you are experiencing anxiety and other painful feelings. When you move toward what's going on *outside your head*, you take control of your retract button.

Congratulations, puppy trainer. You have gained control!

Keep hanging out in the present moment. You'll learn more about that in a bit, but for now appreciate that most worry is future-oriented or past-oriented. When you learn you can bring yourself to the present moment, you find that you're okay. It may not be the best moment of your life, but it is almost always better than where your overthinking mind is taking you.

When you overthink, you are anywhere *but* here and now. Your mind is often in the future, worrying about something that will never happen. This is called a fear fantasy. Or your mind is in the past, rehashing something that happened but distorting the details, because that's what worry does to your ability to think realistically. This is another kind of fear fantasy.

One teen girl says, "The best thing I learned about over-thinking is a saying that 'most of the things you worry about never happen.' So I try to avoid worrying about the future or the past and just concentrate on the present moment. When I'm in the now, I'm being myself."

Being You More Often

Way back at the beginning of this book, Tip 1: Know What You Bring to the Party got you thinking about who you are as a person and what you have to offer others in relationships. Still, the idea of "being yourself" can be confusing because you're still figuring that out. (Even lots of adults are still figuring it out!) It's natural to try on different ways of being you by shuffling things around—like your image, your style, your music choices, your friends, and so on.

Still, at your core, you have a special essence that is yours alone, totally unique, and you can feel that essence flow through you when you are free of self-doubt and anxiety. Think of the last time you really laughed hard. Or the last time you felt really silly, happy, or carefree. Note that you were connected with your essence, your being, uninterrupted and unburdened by overthinking. It was a great feeling, wasn't it?

As you get better at being yourself, you will be able to stay in observable reality instead of getting sucked into a vortex of overthinking. Learning about "triggers" and how they work will help you maintain your power and resist overthinking.

Identify Overthinking Triggers

Sometimes a bout of overthinking seems to take over your mind for no good reason. Often, however, you can examine what triggers your overthinking and keep the puppy close to you before it bounds recklessly into trouble. An example from fifteen-year-old Chloe's life will help you understand how triggers work.

Chloe: It started off to be a perfectly fine day. I went to school, hung out with my friend Kylie during lunch, and headed home to do homework. On my walk home, I shot this text to Kylie, who wasn't in the best mood that day: "Hey, feel better and let's Skype for geometry hw later."

I expected a reply right away, as usual, but didn't receive one. Not getting an immediate reply triggered my overthinking. It wasn't the worst bout of overthinking I ever had, but it was bad enough to cause "zaps of anxiety."

I rationally knew it was no big deal to not get a reply, but Kylie was in a weird mood all day, so I started to wonder if she had a problem with me. I started picking apart how she'd been acting toward me, looking for evidence that she didn't like me, and I felt worse and worse. I've done this a million times in my life, and it just sucks to be paranoid and insecure.

By the time I got home from school, I bit my mom's head off for no reason and was in a full-blown bad mood. I went in my room, slammed the door, made my mom mad at me for being a brat, and then heard my phone chime. Kylie had left her phone in her locker and had to go back to school to get it. I put myself in a bad mood plus I made my mom mad at me for nothing.

Deactivate Triggers

As with Chloe, small events, such as not getting a timely reply from a friend, might trigger a flare-up of overthinking. Making a list helped Chloe identify the following triggers:

Chloe's Triggers for Overthinking

* Not getting immediate replies when texting or social media messaging

* Seeing stuff on social media that makes me feel left out or jealous or not as good as other people

* Friends being in bad moods or acting weird and taking that personally

* Meeting new people, wondering if I'm acting okay

Interpret Reality with Care

Notice that Chloe's triggers are everyday events, which is often the case with teen girls. Also notice how none of the triggers is a problem on its own. It's Chloe's *interpretation* that makes the event negative. We are always interpreting reality around us—and as a teenager, you are more likely to interpret things as being against you, in a personal way. This is normal, and it will get better as you grow older.

Imagine how Chloe's day would have unfolded differently if she interpreted the event this way: "Kylie always texts back right away. There's probably a reason why she's not responding right now. I guess I'll find out."

On her list, Chloe also listed "friends in bad moods" and "taking that personally" as overthinking triggers. In her case, a small event (not getting a timely reply from Kylie) triggered a flare-up of overthinking. Have you ever been triggered like Chloe?

Your Turn: Identifying and Deactivating Your Triggers

Think about what triggers you and write down your triggers on a piece of paper or in your tips notebook.

Take a look at your list of triggers. Can you see how taking ordinary events personally triggers overthinking? Life gets much better when you begin to note your triggers and generate more realistic possibilities for why something is happening, instead of getting sucked into a fear fantasy.

When you come up with different possibilities for what's going on, you think more creatively, positively, and rationally. There is nothing wrong with being emotional, as long as you remind yourself that strong emotions often distort your interpretation of reality. That's why you begin making distinctions between what actually happened (observable reality) and what your fear-based interpretation wants you to believe (fear fantasy).

Let's revisit Chloe's list. Underneath each listed trigger, Chloe came up with another explanation for the event that triggered her and added thoughts and ideas based on observable information. Instead of coming up with all the possible fear fantasies she could imagine, Chloe stuck with the evidence and simplified her interpretations.

Chloe's Triggers for Overthinking—Deactivated

* Not getting immediate replies when texting or social media messaging.

    There is no evidence that Kylie has a problem with me and there was nothing to indicate Kylie's mood was about me. Usually, Kylie's moods have nothing to do with me and that's most likely true now. Regarding not getting immediate replies when texting, there are literally a million reasons a friend may not text right back. I am learning to stop myself from jumping to the worst possible conclusion.

* Seeing stuff on social media that makes me feel left out or jealous or not as good as other people.

    I know that what I see on social media is often constructed for other people and is not as amazing as it appears to be. People are putting effort into showing off their "amazing lives," and I have to remember that. As far as being left out goes, I don't include everybody in everything, and it doesn't mean I don't like the person who isn't there. This is not personal. If I feel left out, I need to make more effort with those girls so that we can plan things together.

* Friends being in bad moods or acting weird and taking that personally.

    There are a million reasons to be in a bad mood, and it most likely has nothing to do with me. I need to trust my friends to let me know if I've done something to put them in a bad mood, or if I feel like it, I'll just ask them directly.

* Meeting new people, wondering if I'm acting okay.

    It's natural to feel self-conscious when you meet new people. I'm not as transparent as I feel, and most people will have no clue how I'm feeling. I will retract the leash on my puppy when I start to overthink about how I'm coming across so that overthinking doesn't keep me from being myself and connecting. I need to remind myself that other people are not extremely focused on everything I say and do. They are either in the moment connecting or they are overthinking themselves!

Anytime you catch yourself overthinking, practice deactivating your triggers to back the puppy away from the skunk, so to speak. If you prefer, you can do it in your head and skip the writing.

Special Trick: When you struggle to come up with more realistic thoughts, access clear thinking by tapping into what you would say to a friend if she came to you upset by the exact same situation. This will help you shake off emotion that is getting in the way of accessing a more realistic viewpoint.

Redirecting the Puppy

Now that you've pulled back your mind, like a puppy it wants something new to focus on—something to occupy its attention. Here is a menu of possibilities you can explore and add to. Try some or all of these redirection strategies so that your mind has the proper training to keep it out of trouble.

The Talk-Back Special

This is an excellent menu choice. The talk-back special involves talking to the puppy—which means, of course, talking to yourself, but in a good way.

The part of your mind that generates fear and worry gets a lot of respect *if* you listen to it. And really, why listen to it? All worry involves the same basic message: "Things are not okay or they weren't okay or they aren't going to be okay. You can't trust yourself and/or other people."

That is not a helpful message. It only makes you miserable worrying about things that probably won't happen, *or if they do* happen, they won't be as bad as you think. Worst-case scenario, something yucky happens—you deal with it in that future moment.

When your puppy approached the skunk, you dealt with it. Worry for days or weeks before your skunk encounter would not have helped you. You made the best decision you could *in the moment* and you got through it. That is a great metaphor for other challenges. Trust that worry will not protect you. You will protect yourself and handle the challenge the best you can in the moment.

You can talk back to worry silently, without anyone knowing what you're doing. Feel free to get sassy or even rude because you are allowed to bully this "bully" right back in the talk-back special. That's the point! Here are some examples:

Fearful thought: *Ack! I was so awkward in that conversation with Sadie. I can tell she doesn't like me.*

Talk-back special: *Uh oh, I feel strong self-doubt. Wait, I'm not going to be bullied by thoughts of self-doubt right now. Go away, self-doubt! Take a hike, overthinking! I give myself permission to feel awkward— it's not a big deal unless I allow my mind to stay focused on it.*

Fearful thought: *Three of my friends posted a picture of themselves over the weekend and I wasn't invited. Do they like me? Did they purposely leave me out? Did they talk about me behind my back?*

Talk-back special: *Oh, it's you again, Worry. You bore me! You can't make me doubt myself. I'm not going to spend my day thinking thoughts given to me by you. I'm not interested in all the insecurity you want to give me. As far as I know, everything is fine with me and those friends, and I'm going focus on what I experience to be true instead of on what I fear might be true. I trust the evidence more than I trust fear-based thoughts.*

You may want to follow up the talk-back special with the here-and-now healer (see below) and learn more about being in the moment.

The Here-and-Now Healer

Let's talk more about being here *now*. If you walk your puppy close to you, it still has plenty to look at and explore. Sure, that skunk up ahead looks interesting, but we know it's trouble. Instead of looking up the path, what would it be like to check out and explore right where you are? In this very moment? Doing so is what we call the here-and-now healer.

Pulling your mind into the present moment, away from stinky, skunky thoughts, is a great way to heal the stress that comes with overthinking. The more you practice being in the here-and-now, the more you are in your body, in the world, in the moment—and not in your head. Here are some tricks to help you:

Shake awake. When you're in your head, you're often not at all in your body. Your body may even feel frozen or hollow, as if you're totally disconnected to it. Some girls say they feel like they are almost entirely in their own heads when they over-think, detached from their physical bodies. Shake, dance, jump, wiggle, stretch, do a yoga pose you make up, fall out of it, do *anything that feels good.* Reunite with your body and give your overthinking mind a rest.

Dive into five. When you're in the moment, you're in touch with your physical experience. When you feel sucked into mental tangles of overthinking, dive into your senses by doing something that involves them:

* **Listen:** Listen to the sounds around you. How many different sounds can you identify? Pretend you have a listening superpower and get really, really focused on your sense of hearing.

* **Smell:** Tune into smells around you or seek out soothing smells, and focus your mind on every

detail of the experience. Take a sniff of everything around you and appreciate the most subtle smells.

* **Touch:** Shift your attention to your sense of touch and seek out contact with textures or experiences that soothe you, such as petting an animal, snuggling luxuriously into the sweatshirt you're wearing, feeling wisps of your hair on your face or neck, interlacing your hands together and appreciating every sensation involved.

* **See:** Open your eyes and really see what's around you—the colors, shapes, and textures; the faces, bodies, buildings, trees. Notice as many details as you can.

* **Taste:** Seek out a soothing taste such as chai tea or a cup of soup—or maybe a refreshing taste like a mint or some lemonade. Enjoy whatever it is as slowly as you can, paying attention to every detail of your experience.

Engage Your Senses and Rest Your Mind

Many teens have been successful in finding new ways to focus on their experiences and engage their senses. Here are some of their ideas:

Celeste: Pet your dog, cat, iguana, the neighbor's hamster, whatever you can get your hands on. Play with clay, Silly Putty, or a fidget toy of some kind. Brush your hair, take a shower, drink a cold glass of water or a warm cup of tea.

Pet the animal with focused, loving intention, and you'll both feel happier. Focus completely on what you're doing and how it feels. Release unrelated thoughts. This takes practice, but you can do it and when you do, your hot spot cools and you feel better.

Mandi: Eat a snack and concentrate on only one bite at a time. Close your eyes and completely focus on that bite and your chewing until it's completely swallowed and gone. It puts you in the moment, plus you realize how often you do things like eat on autopilot, without any appreciation of the experience you're having.

What Mandi describes is called "mindful eating." She learned about mindful eating in a meditation lesson one of her teachers taught in school. Anything you do with focus and attention can become a form of meditation called "mindfulness meditation." Catherine has more ideas.

Catherine: Take a walk and feel your feet hit the ground. Really pay attention to how your body feels. Look around you while feeling your body move.

Some girls especially love doing this in nature and soaking up the good vibes of the natural world around them. Imagine negativity falling off your body as you move, and imagine your body soaking up healing energy around you.

Your Turn: Create Your Menu of Options

Using the ideas above as inspiration, come up with some of your own. One teen girl added knitting to her list, noting that tuning in to the feel of the yarn and the sound of her knitting needles helped decrease her overthinking.

Pay attention to activities that help calm your mind and create a good, solid list—a personalized menu of options you can chose from. Write your list on a piece of paper or in your tips notebook.

Get Creative: Ways to Heal Your Overthinking

Little girls have lots of opportunities to be creative, and they spend a lot of time in imaginative activity. Since teen girls have less time and fewer opportunities, they often miss the connection they used to have with creative play and creative projects. Bring that connection back! Creativity is great for your soul, and it's a wonderful healer for overthinking.

Also good fun for your mind are creating stories, exploring ideas, inventing hairdos, making collages, decorating cupcakes, and trying online craft ideas. Here are some other creative ideas teens have enjoyed:

* *I redecorate my room in my mind. Since there are no budget restrictions, I get very creative.*

* *I collage and use different themes to inspire each collage. For example, if I want to collage my best self, I look through magazines and cut out anything that just makes me feel good—either 'cuz I like it or it feels like me in some way. I like making the collage and looking at it afterward.*

* *I imagine being a professional party planner, and I create elaborate parties in my mind. They are so detailed and creative that now I write them down and put them in a binder. It's fun for me, and it gives me something creative to do when I start worrying or feeling bad.*

* *I think of people I've encountered during the day. I make up stories about their home lives or I think about who they will be in ten years. This works great when I'm trying to fall asleep.*

Puppy Progress

Good for you! You have now graduated puppy training class and are on your way to enjoying a well-behaved puppy. (Whoop-whoop!)

While you enjoy your progress, remember that your mind—and your puppy—continue to be full of life. Because it is the nature of the human mind to be active, creative, and lively, there will be times when your mind wants to overthink. Now that you know more, you will be able to notice bouts of anxiety-provoking overthinking and switch it out for new, better-feeling options. You have a great start, so keep it up, enjoy, and *be* on your way to our final chapter, Tip 10: Learn to Balance!

Just-For-Fun Quiz: Mystery Social Skill

Find out how strong you are at this mystery social skill and get tips for improvement. For each question, select the answer that best fits you and write it on a piece of paper or in your tips notebook.

1. Someone in your life is going through something really rough. You feel the need to

    A. make contact and let them know you're there for them.

    B. give them space, but keep them on your radar with your good thoughts.

    C. steer clear—you have no idea how you could possibly help.

2. You're waiting in a long line behind a girl about your age. She turns around in an animated and friendly way and starts chatting you up about the crazy, terrible day she's having. You most likely to

    A. enjoy the brief interaction, giving yourself permission to just listen and not say much.

    B. wish she'd turn around because she's making you uncomfortable.

    C. listen with interest and offer some words of understanding.

3. You go into the restroom at school and there is a girl you recognize from one of your classes wiping tears out of her eyes and fixing her smeared mascara. You

    A. approach her with warm concern.

    B. offer a brief, uncomfortable smile and avert your gaze quickly to give her privacy.

    C. go about your business as if you don't notice.

4. A new student to the school enters your class, looking totally overwhelmed. Your reaction is to

    A. feel glad that you're not her.

    B. smile at her and indicate the empty desk next to you.

    C. sympathize with her vulnerable situation, but not to the point where you'd do anything differently.

5. Two people you care about are fighting. You want to

   A. stay out of it.

   B. offer support to both parties with the goal of helping them work it out.

   C. offer support, but you're unsure how to go about it, so you wait to see if either person confides in you.

SCORING

Add up your points.

1. A = 5 B = 3 C = 1

2, A = 3 B = 1 C = 5

3. A = 5 B = 3 C = 1

4. A = 1 B = 5 C = 3

5. A = 1 B = 5 C = 3

16–25: You are a warm hug.

That means you are naturally inclined to connect with people and offer words of comfort. If you're closer to 16 than to 25, you are motivated to be there for people. You're growing more confident in putting yourself out there to connect as a supportive friend. If you're closer to 25, people come to you for support and comfort because you're a natural. *Take Note:* If you are in this category, connecting to others with compassion is a valuable quality and skill that you bring to your social world!

11–15: You have a warm heart.

You notice emotional dynamics and you definitely care about what other people are going through. You just aren't sure what you can do about it.

Sometimes you wish you could connect and offer help, but you find yourself holding back. *Take Note:* Your compassion is a great quality that you bring to the party! Try expressing your compassion by offering small gestures of encouragement and support to people around you. Trust yourself, and don't feel shy about expressing your caring feelings more often. Getting good at this will come naturally to you, and other people will appreciate it!

5–10: You are ready to build confidence in yourself as someone who can be there for others.

You prefer to let other people take care of their own issues. It's not that you don't care. It's that you aren't comfortable with that kind of interaction, and you're not sure how to go about connecting with others on that level. You find yourself feeling either stressed or disconnected when other people are struggling. *Take Note:* It would be great for you to experiment getting more comfortable with feelings. Notice your own and other people's, and practice feeling relaxed and accepting of all feelings, even if they involve suffering. Know that you don't need to "fix" anyone's feelings. The best gift you can offer yourself and others is your ability to accept all feelings, as well as a willingness to be present in a calm, kind way. The more comfortable you become with feelings, the more this can become a part of you that everyone around you will appreciate!

tip 10

Practice Balance

If you're like most teen girls, balancing school, health, and home responsibilities—all while trying to have a social life—is challenging. Striking a balance feels like attempting a complicated yoga pose you can hold for about a hot second before you lose control.

When you're balanced, you're rocking all your priorities and managing your time superbly. You're not putting off any part of your life; everything is absolutely thriving and everyone is pleased with you. You are meeting expectations by allocating the perfect amount of time and attention to everything. You are even pleased with yourself.

Please note: No teen girl in the history of the world has ever fit the above description. Nor has any other human being.

In the real world, there are times when you're out of balance and certain parts of your life aren't getting enough (or any) attention from you. It's hard avoiding imbalances, because your commitments are constantly fluctuating.

During final exams, for example, studying may mean that everything else goes out the window, including sleep. After exams, you may do a major sleep catch-up only to accidentally snooze right through your sports practice or some other commitment. Your life may feel like a chaotic rotation of focus and neglect. Stressful!

To add to the pressure, parents, teachers, siblings, coaches, and friends all have expectations of you. When you fall short, you may end up hearing feedback like this:

* You could do well in this class if you worked harder.

* You're spending too much time with X; I feel ditched.

* Are you okay? You look tired.

* Are you giving this your all? It doesn't feel like it.

* You're treating home like a hotel. You need to participate more.

* Your progress report arrived today. We need to talk.

* You are so absorbed in your own life, you don't care about anyone else.

* You spend too much time in your room/on your computer/on your phone.

* You care more about your friends than your own family.

Like yoga poses, your ability to keep life in balance does not need to be perfect. And it won't be. If it is, it will only last a minute because that is the nature of life. There will always be some fly buzzing by that distracts you in your moment of balance, turning your graceful swan pose into injured downward dog.

This is so true that yoga teachers often remind students that yoga is a *practice*, meaning it is something to work on (practice) for life. There is no perfection, and mastery is not the goal.

In yoga, practicing is more important than getting the poses "right." In yoga, there is respect for the ever-changing fluctuations in your life and your body.

What if you began cultivating a similar attitude of respect for yourself as you tend to the needs and requirements of your everyday life? Remember, it will be a practice, and mastery is not your goal. Some days, you will feel like all is on track. Other days, you will note that several areas need more attention.

This chapter is dedicated to supporting you as you practice balance and compassionate self-monitoring. To start, let's hear from Grace, who felt anything but gracefully balanced in her junior year of high school.

✳ *Meet Grace, Age 19*

The quote that inspires her:

> *Balance is not something you find, it's*
> *something you create.* —Jana Kingsford

I learned about balance the hard way in my junior year of high school when I had my first boyfriend. Before I met Jake, I had multiple crushes but never an actual relationship. When Jake and I became official, my relationship with him became the happiest part of my life and I got—not obsessed with it, but let's say "very absorbed." At that time, it seemed impossible for me to find the balance I needed.

My classes were hard junior year, the hardest ever, and it was not easy for me to spend much time with Jake because I also took dance and helped my mom drive my little sister around. Anytime I got a chance, I spent time with Jake. We also texted a lot when we weren't together, which drove a lot of people in my life crazy. I didn't realize how rude I was being.

At first, my friends were supportive of my relationship and happy for me, but after a while, I got a weird feeling from them and they seemed cold and uninterested in me. It was easy to kind of ignore what was going on with them because I wanted to be with Jake anyway.

I was with Jake all school year until that May when he broke up with me. It was the hardest thing that ever happened. I feel dramatic saying that now that a couple of years have gone by, but at the time, I was seriously devastated and sure I'd never get over it.

One of my friends found out about the breakup from social media or something, and she reached out to me. I was overwhelmed with relief because I thought my friends would be over me. Actually, some of them were cold for a while, but they got over it and I was able to reconnect with them.

If it wasn't for my friends that year, I don't know how I would have gotten through my heartache. Over time, they told me a little about how it hurt them when I blew them off for Jake, and I was able to listen and apologize. I let them know how grateful I was for their kindness, and we all got closer because of the honesty and realness.

We are actually still good friends, even though we're scattered geographically. I've made new friends in college, and even though I like them a lot, I love my old friends. There is nothing like your friends being there for you when you don't deserve it.

Anyway, that experience changed me in several ways. I'm a better friend because of it, for sure. I am more committed and caring, and I am quick to forgive because I know what it feels like to need forgiveness and get it. It was huge for me and I want to give that to other people.

My best tip for teenage girls is to keep an eye on your priorities even when it's really hard. What seems like a good idea in the moment may not be a good idea in the big picture, and it's the big picture you need to remember so that your life doesn't crash into the ground.

For me, my big picture currently involves working toward my goals and having good relationships. I would advise teen girls to avoid putting all their eggs in one basket—into just one relationship. Or even just one priority, like dance or school. When your focus is on one thing to the exclusion of others, you lose balance and are more likely to feel lost and alone if something changes somewhere.

Figuring It Out

There are many different things in life that can consume your attention and throw you out of balance. In Grace's case, it was a romantic relationship. It is very common for people of all ages to lose balance when they enter a romantic relationship. It's human nature to want to be with someone you have strong feelings for.

On the other hand, it's very common to feel left out when a close friend suddenly has no time for you. Maybe you have been on one end or the other of this scenario. No matter which end you've experienced, remember that everyone struggles with balance.

Feedback vs. Confrontation

In the case of teen girls, friends often feel hurt and rejected when clear communication could have helped. Clear communication is a great skill to use in challenging times. In Grace's case, she could have talked to her friends to let them know she still cared for them, even though she was spending a lot of time with Jake. A little troubleshooting before things get tense can go a long way.

In the case of Grace's friends, they could have talked to her about wanting more of her time. Girls often feel so much dread at the thought of confronting one another that they withdraw and shut down instead of expressing themselves. That may feel like a better option, but it's not because nothing gets resolved.

Instead of confronting a friend who upset you, consider giving that friend feedback. Giving feedback involves sharing your impression (your feedback) about what's going on with another person. It does not involve approaching that person in a hostile or blaming way. Because giving feedback is more respectful, it is often very effective.

> **Example:** *Grace, you know we love you and we're happy for you and Jake. We just want you to know we miss you. Sometimes it's hard to see you with him all of the time because we want you to be with us sometimes.*

Feedback like this could have given Grace the important information and perspective she needed to redistribute her time and attention more evenly. As things turned out, Grace was fortunate that even without a difficult confrontation, her friends were there for her when she needed them. Not all teen girls have Grace's good luck, which puts them in a position of grieving both the romantic relationship *and* the friendships that have taken a hit. Not fun.

In addition to including feedback and clear communication when nourishing friendships and other relationships, it is also important for teen girls to seek clarity for balance in their lives. Let's see what this might mean in your life.

Clarity for Balance

During the teen years, when life is especially full of changing activities, it may be very difficult to find balance. To do so, it is often helpful to evaluate the important aspects of your life by clarifying what you *have* to do and what you *get* to do.

Have Tos and Get Tos

Some aspects of life you can label as "have tos," because they are required. Examples of have tos are school, household chores, basic self-care, and whatever other commitments you have in your life. While joining a club or a sport isn't necessarily a have to, showing up for required practices/games/meetings become requirements once you've chosen to join. You will notice many have tos can also be enjoyable. Just ask the girl who loves calculus or the girl who likes to sing—loudly—while she vacuums.

Other aspects of life you can label as "get tos," because they are things you want to do and may get to do. Many girls report they enjoy these things even more when they have completed their requirements first. These treats may include watching movies or shows, online socializing, napping, hanging out with friends, and whatever else you like to do with your free time.

Balancing the Two "Tos"

It's not uncommon for teen girls to feel so swamped with have tos that there's no time for get tos. The busier you are, the more you can relate to this frustration. It's tricky because, while it's great to have goals and ambitions, if you don't have time for rest and fun, creativity and pleasure, you will end up paying a price.

When you are too busy, you are vulnerable to illness, injury, anxiety, feelings of emptiness and anger, and overall burnout. However, downsizing expectations that you have for yourself—or that other people have of you—can be hard. If you have ever tried to quit a sports team, you can relate to the drama and uncertainty that often involves the whole family.

The opposite problem occurs when teens are so consumed with fun and distraction that they feel like failures in school and other areas of their lives. These teens tend to end up feeling bad about themselves because they aren't creating success in areas of importance, like school or self-care. It takes time and effort to do well at anything, and while fun distractions can be tempting, they don't necessarily move your life forward in a positive way.

Your Turn: Looking at Your Have Tos and Get Tos

Start thinking about your have tos and get tos, and make a list of each on a piece of paper or in your tips notebook.

How do your lists look? If they feel overly full, think about what you can downsize or eliminate. For one high school junior, eliminating babysitting from her have-to list helped free up time for get tos like hanging out with friends. In the summer, when she had more time, she added babysitting back.

For another high school freshman, social networking ate up time she knew she should be giving to schoolwork. A disappointing progress report illuminated the consequences of her balance problem. Putting off checking in with her friends until after homework was complete helped her to rebalance her priorities and feel more productive. She also noted that she enjoyed her social media time more when she felt she had earned it, as opposed to feeling guilty when she procrastinated with her homework.

Balancing Basics

As you may have noticed, important aspects of life are often very different from person to person. One teen girl may put getting straight As at the top of her list, while another would willingly trade a perfect grade for a chance to play varsity volleyball. On your own list, you may even notice that many top priority items today will not make the lineup tomorrow. But some choices have enduring value and continue to be a priority for many teen girls. Here are a few balancing basics for giving priority to your priorities:

Balancing Your Heart

When you have balance in your heart, you are giving and receiving love—with family, friends, animals, and maybe even humanity as a whole. You are connected with your heart and with kindness toward yourself and others.

In previous tips, you have learned about making contact with people, nurturing relationships, and communicating for closeness. When you practice those skills, your heart is in good balance and you feel good.

When you are super stressed out or going through a hard time, balancing your heart may fall off of your radar. When you see that it has, gently steer yourself back to love—for yourself and for others. Love is the best healing force in the world, and practicing love keeps your heart and your life in better balance.

Best buddies Geena and Violet helped find balance when they got together to cook a special dinner for their families. Everyone's heart got a lift from their gesture. A girl named Sally, who noticed she'd left her little sister out of her life lately, added two sister dates a month to her schedule. Both Sally and her sister felt better and closer after the adjustment.

Your Turn: Balancing Your Heart

How are you at balancing your heart overall? What can you do right now to balance your heart? Come up with some ideas that make your heart smile and write them down on a piece of paper or in your tips notebook to give making-them-happen energy and priority in your life.

Balancing Your Mind

When you have a balanced mind, you have a great attitude toward life. You try to think positively by acknowledging the good things in life. You enjoy a comfortable balance of simple pleasures with creative and intellectual engagement. You keep worry and overthinking in check by practicing what you learned in Tip 9: Be More and Think Less.

When you have balance of mind, you give your mind treats like meditating, listening to music that calms you, or reading a good book. You protect your mind from too much media exposure, especially before bedtime. You give your mind plenty of time to turn off by prioritizing sleep and sneaking in a little nap whenever you can. Balancing your mind is good for you because you get smarter when you engage intellectually and you recharge when you rest and practice habits that help you feel calm.

Your Turn: Balancing Your Mind

Review your life overall as well as how you are doing lately with balancing your mind. On a piece of paper or in your tips notebook, write down any good intentions you'd like to remember and work on.

Balancing Your Health

Finding balance through yoga is good for both your body and your mind. Teens who practice yoga say it makes their bodies feel great while helping their minds feel more calm and focused.

If you are interested in yoga, consider finding a class, watching a DVD, or checking yoga out online. Many teen girls notice that even fifteen minutes of yoga a day can make a positive difference in a busy life.

If you have no interest in yoga, there are many other ways to balance your health. Among them are the familiar suggestions to get enough sleep, eat healthy foods, drink plenty of water, go out in fresh air, and pursue regular exercise. Again, if you feel frustrated because you don't always find time for these important aspects of good health, keep in mind that perfection is still not the point. It is a lifelong practice to balance your body by paying attention and making corrections and improvements to your schedule and lifestyle as you go along. When you *practice* balance, you feel much better and so does your life.

Your Turn: Balancing Your Health

Take a look at yourself in terms of how you balance your health. It's natural to go in and out of good and not-so-good health habits. One day you're rocking fruits and veggies, and the next every potato chip in the bag seems to have your name on it. Think about your health habits. What would you like to tweak or adjust? Add or subtract? Write your thoughts on a piece of paper or in your tips notebook.

Balancing School

When you have balance in your school life, you feel engaged with learning and are growing as a person. You remember you won't love every subject, nor will you be amazing at every subject. Like everyone else in the world, you will have subjects you like and feel good at, and subjects you don't like or that challenge (even torment) you. That is normal and natural. Don't judge yourself harshly.

When you have balance in school, you focus on your effort and love for learning more than you focus on your grades. Focusing too much on grades pulls you out of balance, because you will end up getting stressed out, not resting enough, worrying too much, and neglecting all of the elements of your life that create healthy balance and development.

Even more dangerously, you may begin dreading school and losing your love for learning. Dread is a sign that you need to work on balance by focusing on effort, not outcome.

Do you know that many teens go to college every year with extremely high grade point averages from high school only to come home because they're not ready to be there? The problem for these students is not lack of intelligence. The problem is they arrived at college burned out by the lack of balance they suffered in high school. Years of imbalance take a toll. Burnout means joy and inspiration has been smothered by stress and exhaustion.

Practicing balance in your life *now* will help you avoid that fate and will guide you to nurture balance throughout your life. This means keeping an eye on maintaining balance, not just on your grade point average.

Your Turn: Balancing School

What are your thoughts about how you balance school? Think about changes you could make to create more balance. On a piece of paper or in your tips notebook, write down anything you'd like to bring special energy and commitment to.

Balancing Relationships

When you have balance in your relationships, you make time for all the important people in your life. You prioritize quality, which means you engage in conversation and healthy activities that help you connect to nature, to fun, to another's thoughts and feelings, hopes and dreams.

When you have balance in your relationships, you keep an eye on who might be feeling neglected. Often for teens, family members feel hurt and angry because you spend more time with friends, with media, or in your room, instead of with them. It's easy to fall out of balance in your relationships, and it's completely normal.

When you neglect relationships in your life, it's tempting to ignore the issue and avoid the people you know are annoyed. A better choice is to touch base with them, just to let them know you care and are working toward a balance that includes them.

Think of a time you waited for something, like your food at a restaurant. Don't you feel better when the food server touches base with you to say, "The kitchen is a little slow today, but your meal will be out soon"? Acknowledging lack of balance, even when you can't fix it right away, helps other people know that you care.

If you can make a tweak, remember little gestures can go a long way. With family, you will enjoy the time you spend with them more if you make an effort to engage with a good attitude, instead of dread, avoidance, or frustrated meltdowns. It's better to make efforts than apologies and remind yourself that if you weren't important to them, they wouldn't care about spending time with you.

Your Turn: Balancing Relationships

Are there any changes or tweaks you need to make to create more balanced relationships? What are your ideas, and how might those changes improve your life? Write these on a piece of paper or in your tips notebook.

Tip the Scales

Congratulations! You have worked through all ten tips and are already tipping the social life scales in the right direction. You have more knowledge about social and emotional factors that will help your social life, and you have more skills on board to help you feel confident and make things happen.

At the end of the day, remember: *It is the love and intention you put into your life that creates the life you love.*

It all starts with you opening your heart to yourself and other people. *Enjoy!*

Lucie Hemmen, PhD, is a licensed clinical psychologist who specializes in working with teens and their parents in private practice while raising two teen girls of her own, Marley and Daisy. She is author of *Parenting a Teen Girl*, and has written *The Teen Girl's Survival Guide* for girls who identify social stress as a top concern. Hemmen lives and practices in Santa Cruz, CA.